I0767564

THE PAMPHLET OF THE LAST DROP OF WATER:

The Cooperative and the Missed Sustainability

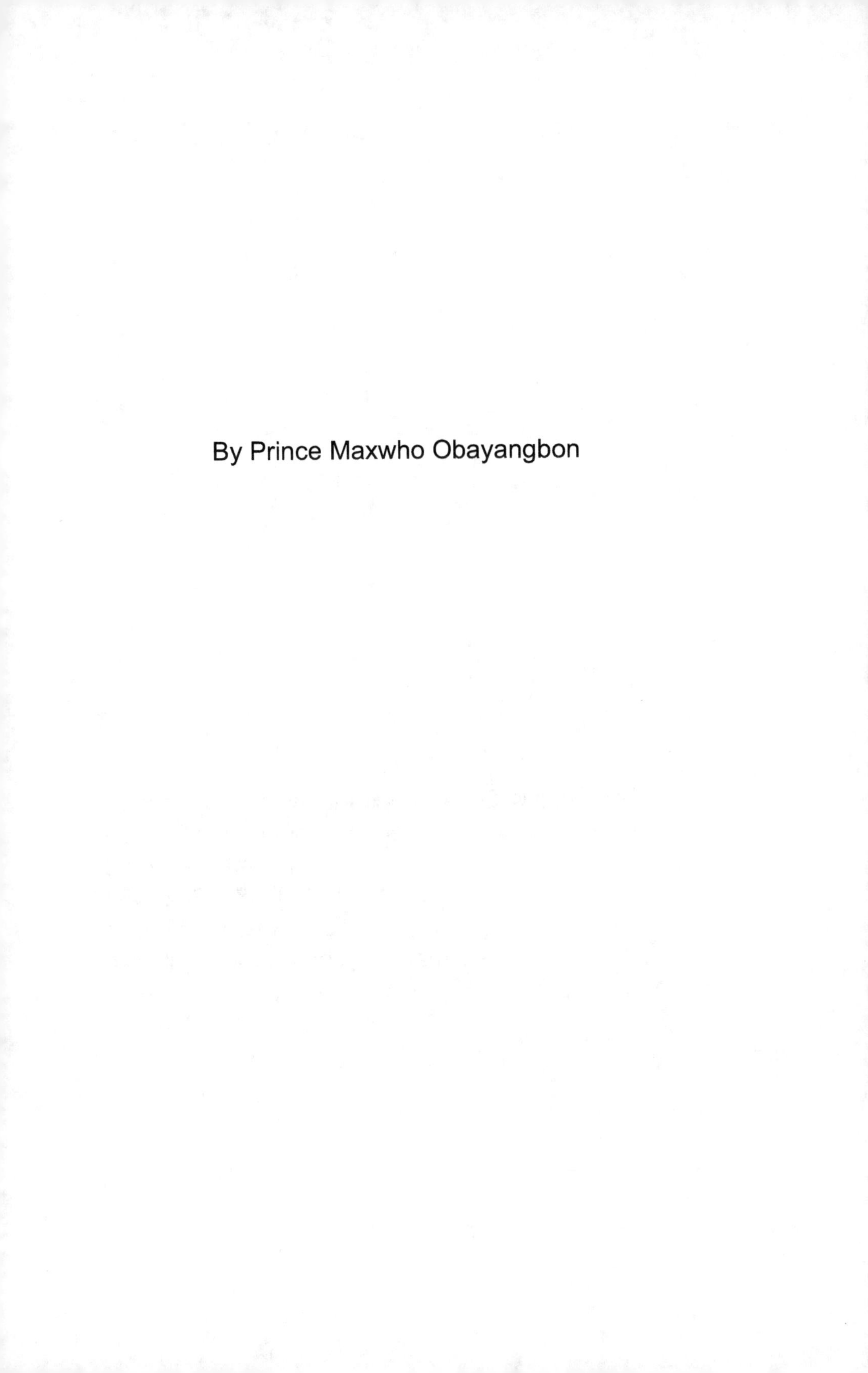

By Prince Maxwho Obayangbon

Contents

DEDICATION

In essence, this current research, presented in the form of a documentary narrative, is dedicated to all social animals and aims to address the distorted cooperative operating system, particularly in Italy. It is deeply rooted in a profound concern for social issues and their principles and fundamental importance, specifically in the aspect of 'social solidarity' in terms of cooperation within a specific community. I am propelled by a strong motivation to actively involve all stakeholders through meaningful interaction, sincere dialogue, and human engagement towards a feasible contribution in the end. Indeed, the ultimate goal is to achieve sustainable results that align with the evolving nature of the social conditions of our times.

Perhaps I have been foolish, or perhaps I have been astute, or perhaps I am simply conforming to the expectations of our society. In any case, I have dedicated myself wholeheartedly to strictly adhere to the moral norms of our society because I have always been aware of the consequences. It is important to acknowledge that I am not alone in this struggle of being conscious of this fact; meaning that many others also find themselves in a similar situation. Recognizing my limitations and capabilities, I am making a conscious effort to navigate my daily routine within these boundaries. It is always a constant battle, but one thing is certain: I am determined with concern for the well-being of those around me, as well as for myself.

To my great astonishment, I have recently discovered that, at this point in life, a significant part of the members of our society seems to have become insensitive to abhorrent acts of oppression, deprivation, humiliation, segregation, racism, and other forms of atrocities against each other in this enigmatic existence of ours. These distressing behaviours are happening right before our eyes or even in our own communities every day. It's as if these attitudes have turned into a deliberate cultural desire among humans.

The apathy to such injustices is deeply worrisome. It is bewildering to see how these once universally condemned actions have now somehow been normalized or overlooked by many. This attitude is becoming a lack of interest in the suffering and mistreatment experienced by others, and in most cases, even while it is being perpetrated by others, which is, in a sense, everyone's pain in disguise, after all.

However, it seems that we either do not discuss this topic enough, or we are only scratching the surface when we do. Even worse, there are cases where we simply choose not to acknowledge or act upon it.

This is particularly unsettling when those in positions of power, who should lead the charge, prioritize their selfishness and short-term personal interests over addressing these crucial issues that concern us all.

It is imperative that we delve into this matter and engage in meaningful conversations about it. By doing so, we can shed light on underlying issues and work towards effective solutions. It is time for those in power to fulfil their responsibilities and actively contribute to positive change rather than being consumed by their fleeting desires. Let us join in the collective effort to construct a society where important issues are not neglected or treated superficially—especially when they concern the needy among us—but addressed with genuine dedication and a long-term perspective.

THE POWER OF GRATITUDE: A Journey of Reflections

I must strongly state that I have learned a lot about collaborative solidarity here in Italy from some special people I have encountered during the challenging moments of my personal life. In particular, I have been deeply impressed by the generosity and assistance received from various teachers and professors at the various schools I attended simply as a student. These distinguished personalities have shown a great sense of compassion and empathy, culturally universal, offering me moral and practical support when I needed them most. Not only did they help me overcome personal difficulties, but they also encouraged me to continue learning and growing despite adversities. I am grateful for the positive impact these people have had on my life.

Overall, over time, I have gained a profound awareness: while most of humanity lives immersed in their own ideology and superficial interests, often ignoring reality in favour of fantastical worlds. From this perspective, every form of human thought could distort the factual evidence of our existential reality. Therefore, I am diligent in evaluating sources of information, aware that knowledge supported by concrete evidence is what matters. So, I have decided to learn from everyone, through the contributions of each, considering the attributes of all without favouring any source.

This means that we, along with everything around us, including you, me, our environment, and our circumstances in this enigmatic existence, are my formidable reference points in writing this book!

"The real fun lies in observing how what I thought was new often had similar roots already present in reality (albeit in a different form or resemblance)." This experience has led me to see myself as a "common man trapped in the midst of the unknown," as a fraction of existence in continuous evolution.

This book is not an intellectual exercise or a celebration of the work of other intellectuals. It represents my personal journey into the world of cooperatives. At this point, I have to confess that I am not a poet or a playwright, but I feel obligated to recount my experience, simply through my consciously reflected vision. Here I try to apply common sense to tangible reality, avoiding scientific dogmatism. My intent is to make understanding accessible to anyone (experts or laypeople), without experience limits. The goal? In other words, is to present a practical approach to understanding our surrounding circumstantial reality without falling into dogma.

If I were to give credit to every source, the words in this book would belong to others and not to me. In fact, I myself am a recipient of the life concept that I share here. I thank everyone who has crossed my path, from YouTube channels to books read, especially my own life. I would like to express gratitude to those who have guided me in my knowledge acquisition journey. This interest was developed from a cultural focus rather than an artistic one, prompting me to undertake this research.

My key to understanding cooperatives and social solidarity, especially in Italy, was witnessing an incongruous way the functions were carried out in this field. So, I took the initiative to create a cooperative with my trusted friends. As a first step, I consulted with an accountant who was in my vicinity. I was fortunate enough to have met a generous 'accountant' who provided me with an anthology on cooperative organization: ('Solidarity cooperatives' Guide to establishment and management, editions of the Gino Mattarelli consortium'), which was a great gift to read before deciding to form a cooperative group. This book fundamentally solidified my understanding of what a cooperative should be, in addition to what I knew through different literatures, my collaboration with various forms of social services, and my general and human conception of social solidarity.

So, if I were truly interested in identifying heroes, I should look among those without a name and without a voice, among the so-called 'unknown soldiers' of collective interest, just like the son of man who had no place to lay his head! My gratitude goes to those who have dedicated their lives to creating a better world, often in anonymity, often without receiving recognition or compensation. Improvements are not the result of the work of a few extraordinary and exceptional individuals noticed by the mainstream, but rather the cumulative work of countless people who have contributed significantly, even in different entities. It is through the commitment of these people put together that we can continue to aspire to a better future.

I am humble and privileged to have had the opportunity to learn and be inspired by these unknown pioneers. Their contributions will be forever remembered and honoured, even with this book.

Today, it is important to note that the individuals I am referring to, most of whom have left no tangible proof or documentation in our history books, are the unknown and the nameless: often not celebrated by official history. However, their contribution can be understood only by spending time with them in their daily lives or observing their actions and behaviours first-hand, or learning through the traces they have left somewhere and somehow; their precious teachings in a more unconventional way that have enriched our present. Let us not forget that heroes often remain nameless.

In conclusion, for the good of all: this experience helps us develop greater empathy and understanding of our natural surroundings, going beyond dominant historical narratives and acting for the good of existence, especially for those and for things that have no voice!

PREFACE

This book is about an analysis of a form of cooperation within the connotation of 'SOCIAL-SOLIDARITY in the formation of COOPERATIVES' in cultural terms. It has been carefully conceived and written in the Italian language with the intention of providing an accurate view of cultural evolution in our days. My choice of choosing the Italian language is not arbitrary but to respond to the desire to capture the authenticity in terms of the communicative nuances and richness of the treated cultural context, which requires the harmonious coexistence of its cohesive elements. Since culture and history of each place impose a form of linguistic expression capable of fully representing the intrinsic behaviour of the actions of individuals who share the same aforementioned elements, united by their complexity and diversity. Therefore, I considered that was essential to adopt this language to ensure accurate and authentic communication with the interest of my readers at heart. In addition, the use of culturally accepted national language also emphasizes the importance of the coexistence of elements that constitute the identity of a defined environment or place in coherency. This linguistic choice reflects the desire to promote an inclusive and respectful dialogue of my narrative among the diverse components of society involved, allowing them to share their experiences and viewpoints effectively.

Through this book, my aim is to offer a significant contribution to the understanding and appreciation of the cultural and linguistic riches inherent in the place in question. I hope that this work can serve as a bridge to greater awareness and mutual understanding among the different facets of this same society. It also examines the highlights of our contemporary society and the collaboration dynamics that characterize it. Its core is the analysis of cooperation without being influenced by specific ideology or linguistic barrier of selfish interest. This perspective constitutes the cornerstone of my analysis.

I want to clarify that I have no intention of harming or proving anything about what is right or wrong (as we all know it in parts and to different extents). In this narrative, what I am trying to do is share what I have learned, especially through my experience collaborating with different cooperatives. I seek to contribute to the investigation of a joint effort to further define, with a loud voice, the concept of "social solidarity": in a factual and cultural context with our actions for survival in relation to sustainability.

Disclaimer: This book is influenced by our cultural conception and the legal framework of our society. It is based on the historical context of the 21st century, so while I am writing it. However, it is important to recognize that my understanding of this situation may evolve over time. This will depend on whether the attitude I am challenging becomes culturally acceptable in the future and becomes justified by our social and collective memory. For me, I believe that every thought, like an argument, must be shaped and be relatively put into consideration with the temporal aspect and the space in which the action or situation is unfolding, to have a critical look or/and obtain a fruitful solution in line with the established objectives.

I must say in advance that I am a verbal communicator in a profane way, not a novelist by nature! Forgive me if I fail to meet the conceptual framework of the traditional approach to writing. Here, I am not trying to support a specific concept of morality but to express my point of view: strictly on the theme of 'cooperation,' 'professional ethics,' and above all 'social solidarity.' That is, this interweaving among us can be sustainable in the long term so that it can persist even in the near future.

The main purpose of this book is to manifest the need for a dialogue between me and those who should have shared my same social valuable goals and objectives; however, I was denied this opportunity during my work experience. I want to assert my current maturity firmly: bellicose logic is no longer a part of me. I am against violence and believe in the importance of resolving conflicts through dialogue and mutual understanding. Peace and cooperation are fundamental to building a better world. This reflection wants to be the tangible product of my sincere desire to express my ideas that, I think, could bring benefits in one way or another to the society of which I am a part of. My goal here is also to stimulate impulses of everyone to contribute virtuously to collaborate for the good of our community 'no matter where', with the perspective of conceiving the term cooperative as an organizational formation for good for all.

This caution is motivated by the desire to preserve the integrity of an impartial and rigorous assessment of the situation. My intention is not to condemn the entire intellectual landscape but rather to raise the important issue of responsibility in the critical evaluation of informative sources. Recognizing this nuanced manipulation of data helps us develop a sharper discernment, to seek the truth with current facts beyond pre-packaged narratives. Only through accurate exploration, careful analysis, and a critical approach can we hope to achieve a more complete and informed understanding of our complex and multifaceted reality. This criticism does not arise from arrogance or disdain for consensus but from my suspicion regarding lies and contradictory historical narratives. This book does not pursue persecutions but invites reflection on how we represent humanity to and between each other. Each episode is a separate argument or a moving phase, as in real life. It concerns human as the protagonist in his natural and cultural environment.

This narration does not deal with ideological, philosophical, or moral issues.

I want to address reality through visible evidence for all. My effort aims to stimulate a collective attitude that could be useful to face the current challenges that society must confront so that social solidarity can be concretized for the good of all humanity. This book arises from my daily reality, lived in my subconscious and conscious mind, but explained without a specific time period, due to human emotions that often influence interpersonal relationships. I will try to select the most relevant episodes, chosen for my expressive ability, both linguistic and cultural, through my stream of consciousness. My new work experience with cooperatives seemed like a dream world, given my intellectual ingenuousness. However, it seemed to me that these organizations (cooperatives) represent a civilization bearing social solidarity within a democracy towards true human subservience, united with a profound awareness of civil rights. In particular, cooperatives should stand out for their ability to involve members in cooperative management, making collective decisions, and promoting economic equality. Thanks to this experience, I have learned a lot about the strength of solidarity and collaboration on my own, which can generate shared and sustainable value for the entire community. My curiosity has turned into my sustenance and my main motivation in all these useful cultural interferences that we have as human beings, constantly interacting with our environment. These interferences are productive for our cultural intellect since they allow us to expand our knowledge of the world and ourselves. In particular, interaction with cultures different from ours enriches us, expanding our perspective and stimulating our creativity. This cultural exchange can be extremely beneficial for all participants, as interaction with diverse cultures enriches and stimulates creativity, fostering mutual understanding and building bridges between communities. In this way, curiosity becomes a driving force for learning and human development. With the sincerity of my heart, I am not trying to convince anyone simply by the information told below. First of all, I would like to state that I do not intend to persuade anyone by the information presented here. I would rather besiege you all to be attentive and diligent in observing your daily reality with adequate human sensitivity in terms of social solidarity for a deeper understanding of the situation narrated in this book. Sometimes, _I might insist on different situations in a tautological or repetitive way, but I want to emphasize that different situations distinguish themselves in the effect they have on our cultural characteristics within civil society_. So please bear with me! Precisely, I must say that before making any information mine, I must first make it accessible to my real activities to test the substance of its existence!

INTRODUCTION

Allow me to introduce myself; my name is Prince Maxwho Obayangbon. I am a simple social being with a degree in Dams (Disciplines of Arts, Music, and Entertainment) from the University of Padua. My interest lies in exploring the cultural process in music production and sound engineering, which primarily represents my profession. In short, I have had various life experiences, shaped by the challenges of growing up alone from a young age. These experiences encompass cultural, academic, and the street education I acquired while living as an adult from time to time.

With humbleness, I stake my claim as a potential trailblazer, possibly the world's inaugural certified conflict manager, as conferred by the title itself. In my forthcoming publication, I intend to delve into the intricacies of effective conflict management, shedding light on the indispensable skills and insights necessary to navigate this domain with finesse. Central to my discourse will be the exploration of prevalent misinterpretations surrounding commonplace lexicon vocabularies, which gradually style our cultural and behavioural norms. It is my firm belief that words such as love, peace, contrast, and others often serve as catalysts for misunderstandings in our social interactions, compelling me to undertake the mission of dispelling these misconceptions.

Beyond the confines of theoretical discourse, my ultimate vision is to play a role in shaping a world where conflicts, irrespective of their nature, are met with compassion and resolved through the application of wisdom. Through the cultivation of a culture rooted in inclusivity and perpetual reconciliation, I aim to lay the foundation for enduring coexistence and harmonious living. This aspiration propels my endeavours as I strive to contribute meaningfully to the collective journey towards a more reciprocal respect and equitable merit in our global society.

Ironically, some individuals in society have labelled me as black, even though my colour is closer to brown than black. I hope my intention is clear. From that precise moment, I stopped believing in what others say about people unless it is supported by clear concrete evidence and intellectually reasonable assessments. I find it important to introduce this preliminary consideration to illustrate the path I intend to take in the next steps.
After a prolonged wait of over seven years, I have finally dedicated my time to delve into the functioning of "social cooperatives" formation in Italy, focusing

especially on our cooperative, drawing from my personal experiences as concrete evidence.

However, I want to emphasize that this does not mean I am an impeccable individual; on the contrary, I am aware of my flaws, which, as is typical for any human being, may be associated with me in a peculiar way. Nevertheless, I am deeply convinced that any objective originating from progressive dialogue, sharing, humility to admit one's shortcomings, and the willingness to correct oneself for the good of all existence becomes a vital attitude in building a viable society.

Throughout this journey, I have had the opportunity to accumulate valuable experiences through my daily life, work, and immersion in social contexts oriented towards our common good. This growth process has been further enriched through in-depth studies, guided by my own vulnerability, and with the goal of contributing to the good of humanity.

Since 2014, I have found myself playing a full-time role as a cultural and linguistic mediator, working closely with cooperatives, prefectures, courts, and hospitals. Before undertaking this journey together, I want it to be clear that every argument will be based on social issues. We must clearly define our goal, which represents the guiding thread of this journey and is the central theme of this book.

I want to emphasize that I do not intend to support utopian theories but rather present tangible facts based on my direct experience. Let's start by asking ourselves: what is our priority and goal in the "social" field, between the following two alternatives?

1) The establishment of the "cooperative" with the aim of feeding oligarchic elites, or

2) The promotion of a society that creates favourable living conditions for all citizens of this nation, thus contributing to the achievement of the goal of "social solidarity" and collective well-being?

This book was written with the intention of supporting the second option presented above, in accordance with the constitutional principles of the Italian Constitution, in Article 45, which unequivocally states: "The Republic recognizes the social function of cooperation of a mutual nature and without purposes of private speculation. The law promotes and encourages its increase by the most suitable means and ensures its character and purposes with appropriate controls."

In a curious intertwining of events, I found that the reality of many cooperatives operating in our territory contradicts the ideals stated by the Constitution. On the contrary, during my journey in the sector, I encountered individuals who, despite their apparent simplicity, concealed dark and opaque aspects.

Personally, I would never have imagined that this dynamic would develop in reality so eloquently, almost imitating the representation of a 'comedy of Art,' where a democratic structure would prove vulnerable and fragile, subject to the manoeuvres of screenwriters and actors acting on behalf of oligarchic elites.

I ask everyone for permission to start this journey into the world of cooperation with you, through the concept of 'solidary' designation. Although it may seem like a dream, it is a reality that is an achievable goal if we collaborate. The solidary designation is based on the idea of supporting local communities, sustainable economies, and human solidarity. In this way, we can contribute to promoting social justice and environmental sustainability.

I am excited about the idea of starting this new adventure together with those who are interested, and it is with great enthusiasm that I am about to discover how we can truly make a difference through the power of cooperation and solidarity. However, I would like to address a preliminary issue.

Whether I accept it willingly or not, whether I find myself in agreement or disagreement, the reality clearly emphasizes that for more than three decades that I have been living in this country. This reality is the focal point to which I refer, and I cannot deny that I unconditionally belong to this same society, that is, to the Italian community. It is in this context that I have been able to obtain most of these indispensable tools for my knowledge acquisition process and also for my survival, which was also as a result of demanding sacrifices.

For these reasons, I have decided to express some considerations regarding the concept of social solidarity, a fundamental premise for the establishment of any form of cooperation. My reflections on various aspects of this subject have no intention of serving as condemnation of anything. It is undeniable that the voices of my conscience are reflected only through the evidence of my existence and within the confinement of the rule of law.

It is because of this that in my narration, I do not aim to reproduce others' texts verbatim, nor do I quote phrases or individual words. I firmly believe that creativity and originality are indispensable pillars of an authentic and effective story. Furthermore, I do not intend to endorse what my conscience does not endorse and of which I do not possess tangible evidence.

It is crucial to remain faithful to our values and principles, even in the course of writing. Only in this way can we manifest authenticity and convey a message that fully reflects our essence and factual perspective.

I ardently hope that my story can serve as a positive contribution to the world I belong to, inspiring others to follow the dictates of their conscience and to act with integrity.

In this book, I want to address aspects related to humanity through the lens of my direct participation, as well as those elements that, at the same time, have caused me deep discomfort: everything connected to my sensitivity to cultural issues within an evolving society. What I am about to describe represents how I have personally perceived and experienced my journey within this cooperative system.

Of course, it should be emphasized that other individuals may perceive these experiences differently, without necessarily delving into deep reflections on them. In order to adequately prepare those who are about to immerse themselves in this narrative related to my experience in the cooperative world, it is important to emphasize that this story is based on the flow of my consciousness, without being bound by temporal or spatial conventions. All events I will narrate took place during those years spent in the field of social solidarity, a topic that I had initially not planned to explore.

I have a deep passion for the literature and philosophy of cooperation and social solidarity, yet, despite my expectations generated by my theoretical study of these concepts, I experienced great disappointment while trying to live the reality. This disappointment was the result of my surrendering affection to the illusory abode of social provision. The experience turned out to be one of the most painful and significant of my life's journey, as you will learn later in this book.

My "intellectual naivety" led me to believe in the supposed goodness of humanity in some people, a belief that turned out to be extremely flawed. This book could actually be considered a form of verbal catharsis stemming from my inability to act differently to influence a situation that I deeply judge as inhumane. After years of futile attempts to establish constructive dialogue with the stakeholders, I felt a growing frustration that found an outlet through these pages.

I usually don't dedicate myself to denouncing injustices perpetrated against people considered "normal," as these individuals can fight for their rights. However, when it comes to individuals who, due to their intrinsic inability to compete (such as the differently-abled), are disadvantaged, I consider such injustices a grave offense against all of humanity. In these circumstances, it becomes a moral obligation for every capable individual to defend the rights of those who cannot do so for themselves, just as we take responsibility for protecting children entrusted to our care due to their vulnerable nature.

It remains important to reiterate that this book does not aim to preach a utopian theory for equality for all. Furthermore, it must be strongly emphasized that I do not intend to support a cause for able-bodied individuals. On the contrary, my intention is to promote the defence of those among us who cannot comprehend, desire, or ask for anything other than guidance and support. These individuals are devoid of words and voice in every chapter of their existence; in simpler terms, they are individuals with various forms of disabilities, often defenceless but capable of feeling pain, shedding tears, and, above all, possessing the vitality that characterizes them as being part of the very fabric of our humanity.

In this textual narrative, I will exert the utmost care to avoid any form of ambiguity in the correspondence between words and meanings. I will try to avoid any slippage towards rhetoric, as this could lead to misunderstandings regarding issues related to cultural formation. In particular, I want to emphasize that I do not wish for this testimony to fall into inaccuracy. It is an important clarification, as the arts of writing, painting, and verbal interaction were also born as means to escape, even if for a moment, our complex and enigmatic reality.

Yet, in the current context, we sometimes find ourselves confused precisely because of evasive statements that are mistakenly interpreted as firmly anchored to reality. Instead, it is reality itself that I wish to address carefully in this narrative. Initially, I tried to banish every cliché and any metaphysical speculation to avoid any preconception in the face of the events unfolding before me. Before anything can be misunderstood, I want to clarify that I consider the idea underlying the creation of cooperatives as one of the brightest sociological discoveries of humanity, one that has been acclaimed for its ability to promote mutually beneficial relationships, understood as interactions among existing and non-existing beings, regardless of gender. I did not intend to transcribe a long story, but I found myself compelled by my fervour for socio-cultural knowledge and the desire to focus on the good of humanity through research. This prompted me to bring to light deceptive attitudes towards those considered 'needy.'

The goal of this book is not to pass judgment but to gain awareness regarding the path we are treading and to define the appropriate path to achieve authentic social solidarity with humanitarian obligations, which should represent our supreme purpose.

To further clarify my position on solidarity among living beings, perhaps unwittingly embedded in my daily actions, I diligently tried to base my statements on the reality of facts. I made an effort to remain consistent with my conscience in the face of what is called "truth," a reality always subjective within the enigma itself that constitutes "life," a reality that is by nature fleeting and elusive.

Here we are: PRELUDE

My Experiences and Reflections

This is my story, a narrative that commenced with assumptions that continue to perplex me deeply today. My journey has been characterized by extensive collaboration with various social-oriented associations and state-managed assistance and healthcare programs. I engaged with different associative organizations, notably with this cooperative, where I served as a member and worker for about seven years. My primary role was that of a cultural and linguistic mediator, although I also worked in other social fields. Thus, I was employed in this cooperative as an untrained operator. To provide some background, I hold a degree from an Italian university. I am an artist in the commercial music genre, a member of the 'BlackMachine' group, where I serve as a producer, author, and singer. Additionally, I've had the opportunity to travel worldwide, encountering various cultural situations. I am proficient in more than two languages, including Italian and English. The cooperative invited me to work based on my reputation as someone who had consistently collaborated with different organizations as a cultural and linguistic mediator. It was evident that the cooperative's leaders needed someone with my skills and experiences. However, I was hired at a lower level, which had a negative impact on me. Another aspect that troubled me was the employment of the president's daughter and the Godfather of one of his sons. They secured higher job positions than mine, despite lacking my qualifications and experience in the specific sector they were employed in. At the time, I interpreted this as a discriminatory attitude, even against me, a manifestation of prevailing racism in this part of the world. However, it is important to emphasize that I chose this job not only for the compensation but also for an element that I perceived as deeper within the world of cooperatives at the time – 'solidarity.'

Initial Impressions on Dynamics in the Cooperative and Revelations

Before being called to work as a cultural and linguistic mediator, I had always believed that cooperatives played a fundamental role in society, aiming to promote and maintain social well-being in a given community. However, my experience proved otherwise. This disheartening discovery compelled me to feel the urgency to share what I had experienced. This pamphlet represents my personal testimony and the narration of events that I can no longer keep to myself. I intend to expose everything clearly and precisely, preserving the integrity of my conscience. I sought constructive dialogue with the cooperative's administrative body, but in the long run, it proved to be fruitless or at least challenging. So, I decided to make my opinions public, not to establish who is right or wrong, but to encourage thoughtful reflection and potential social growth for the well-being of all. This is my intention. There are always individuals who feel entitled to criticize others' beliefs without providing opportunities for discussion or verifying facts before accepting the validity of their hypotheses. This attitude often stems from a lack of clarity in facts, leading to speculation instead of rational explanations. Sometimes, it could be caused by the limited ability to analyse complex events that require a logical or bureaucratic explanation. Moreover, the fear of losing our current status of survival could contribute to this phenomenon.

It may be surprising that wars are everywhere, fought in different ways and for different reasons, whose causes seem to be immediately recognizable. In reality, the deep causes of these conflicts lie in the accumulation of small mistakes made every day, both consciously and unconsciously, ignoring common interests in favour of ephemeral and insignificant ones. Some people are working so hard that wars become almost inevitable, due to widespread pettiness, where many derive satisfaction from others' misfortune, motivated by selfish gain and vanity. Personally, I believe that every reasonable decision, especially in a group context, should stem from open discussion among different opinions. Often, when we develop an idea, we tend to think it's the best. However, by interacting with others, we can understand that their suggestions might be more convincing and enrich our thinking. This is why I have always considered dialogue as an essential tool for personal growth, intellectual evolution, and the creation of meaningful projects. I also believe that an idea remains only a vague intuition until it is tested in reality, with the comparison of other ideas. This observation taught me that the distance between an idea and its implementation can be considerable, and only thorough examination can validate its feasibility. Relying on premature certainty without a 360-degree evaluation can be dangerous and misleading. Indeed, science promotes the complete verification of facts through questioning, investigation, and evidence collection. In scientific inquiry, precise and accurate data is fundamental, as small errors can lead to incorrect deductions. The scientific method carefully evaluates hypotheses and theories through rigorous experimentation and validation. This process of verification and experimentation is crucial to expanding knowledge and developing a deeper understanding of our world. Therefore, validation through verbal discussion emerges as the secret weapon of any form of cooperation. However, in modern societies, hypocrisy is often entrenched in this aspect, and combating it is essential to ensuring authentic communication among people.

We have always criticized the cumbersome bureaucracy that afflicts society, but it is important to recognize that the inefficiency of social processes is often fuelled by incompetent officials resistant to innovation for trivial reasons. This underlying hypocrisy has strengthened my desire to write this pamphlet, with the aim of highlighting how the current society is characterized by incongruities, where often what is preached does not find reflection in actions.

Different Opinions Before My Decision to Write

It took a long time before I could finally start writing this book, for a particular reason linked to the mentality rooted in our culture, even among friends who show me affection. They were afraid that openly expressing my opinions could lead to retaliation from the holders of power in our time. It is not the first time I have tried to promote an attitude of social correctness, a challenge that could turn against those who propose it. Many people advised me to stay away from these topics to avoid personal trouble. Some warned me of a position of vulnerability, while others, with religious motivation. However, I also discussed this issue of selfish enrichment with serious friends who are cohesive in the principles of social solidarity. Their reaction revealed how deep the problem was, pushing them towards personal considerations about the prevailing selfishness in the usual context. The criticisms raised, therefore, led me to examine the information related to this situation. Surprisingly, I found that much of the fragmentary information from my colleagues was often the result of collective gossip, accepted without verification. The deemed unquestionable information was mainly based on assumptions, highlighting a preference for superficial information, easier to understand, requiring less energy and knowledge. Moreover, the people involved were not surprised by my perception of the situation. In fact, many of them justified the attitude with a "that's how the world goes, you have to adapt to the system to survive here." This led me to consider this circumstance as a challenge, pushing me towards a more in-depth study and offering a learning opportunity. There were no shortages of those who declared that nothing could be done about it, claiming that it had always been that way. Even by explaining in detail the situations I had observed and heard, I could not avoid the reaction being a laugh. It seemed that they had already encountered or heard about similar situations, without being able to connect all the elements into a clear explanation of antisocial behaviour. Too often, these situations survive thanks to gossip, regardless of truth. One of the main reasons that prompted me to write this book is the desire to highlight honest people within the system. People who have exceptional potential and contribute to the common good through solidarity. If we remain silent in the face of the attitude towards the less privileged of humanity, we become accomplices to this injustice. *The people who warned me were trying to protect me, but they were actually abandoning humanity to its fate. They selfishly forgot that we are all part of the same humanity, and I consider myself just a part of existence, like a tree that alone cannot form a forest.* For them, the best solution seemed to be to adapt to the system, resigning themselves to the idea that change was impossible. This presumptuous attitude, which presumes to know everything without reflection, deeply concerns me. In some way, I see a correlation between this decline in culture and the invasion of technology into our daily lives, progressively distancing us from real human relationships. So, I took a step forward and began talking to colleagues and companions about this undemocratic and inhuman system, which was supposed to be a pillar of trust and social honesty but actually had shortcomings. The response was often an assumption: "It has always been like this and will continue to be." I realized that when knowledge does not push in a sharp way, it does not influence our lives, and it does not motivate us to progress towards recognition goals. Is this the reality of cooperatives for social solidarity? I invite all of you to share the brief narrative of my stay in the land of Cooperatives.

Beginning of the Narrative and My Reflections

One day, like many others, marked the start of this story—a day unfolding dynamically according to the design of the "power of creation." Every day, I learn to navigate the system called life, trying to maintain control within the possibilities offered by that same "cosmic unity" that is the human condition. In the early summer of 2015, a phone call shattered the monotony of my routine. On the other end of the line, a stranger introduced himself so warmly and familiarly, as if we were long-lost friends. The appointment in question was about a job as a "linguistic and cultural mediator." He identified himself as an associate member of a cooperative called... The purpose of the meeting was their Reception Centre for immigrants and refugees and their need for collaboration. I wanted to know how he got my phone number; he replied that someone working in another similar organization had provided it. Until that moment, I had worked as a linguistic and cultural mediator, offering my services more or less for free to help organizations and public offices.

However, I hadn't been convinced to work with any of them due to impressions of their organizational and structural approach, as well as financial aspects. The entire system, as far as I was concerned, did not seem innovative and adequate to promote a progressive cultural interaction truly helpful in building a cohesive society. It's important to emphasize that these observations weren't judgments or criticisms but reflected my perception of a missing cultural aspect in today's society's approach. I refer to the irrational approach to the situation, where financial goals often prevail over building meaningful and coherent relationships. So, with a friendly aura, I agreed to meet this gentleman the next day. We chose a bar near my house. During the meeting, I shared my opinions with him, and he did the same. It was evident that he, too, hoped to make a difference, just like me. The meeting was fruitful and enjoyable, paving the way for future collaborations. He invited me to visit their main headquarters.

My First Impression of the Office

The atmosphere in the headquarters' office of the cooperative felt familiar, with a warm attitude and genuine smiles on everyone's faces. At that moment, I could never have imagined that the entire framework revolved around a single individual, not for his competence but for his political desire to become the sole beneficiary of the structure's affairs, both financially and influentially. This was how I entered the world of true cooperatives—a journey that would reveal the most extraordinary dark side of reality. On that occasion, another individual was introduced to me: a thirty-year-old, eloquent, and full of brilliant ideas in the social field. Later, I discovered that he, too, had recently been hired by the cooperative. After our meeting, I was also immediately recruited.

My Integration into the Cooperative

The motive was very clear why they sought me out: they needed my expertise in cultural interactions and social contexts, which they weren't adequately prepared to handle outside their presumed theatrical or theoretical preparation and the bureaucratic formalities necessary for participating in the tender relative contracts. Despite my university education and the skills gained in my previous work experiences, I was hired at the lowest regulated structural position, that of the untrained operator. This was a blow to me, but my dedication to being of help to the society hosting me and the needy people kept my motivation alive. During that time, the cooperative was launching a reception project for immigrants. Initially, they had only one apartment to accommodate the first 5 Gambian refugees, a number which was destined to grow exponentially over time.

Organization of the Cooperative at First Glance

Unfortunately, a disagreement among the apartment's guests turned into a violent struggle. Regrettably, the issue was not handled accurately, necessitating the intervention of the law enforcement agency to resolve the situation, followed by arrests and judicial persecution. This event put the cooperative in a difficult situation, which is why I was hired as a member. I spent my first years of work focusing on how the cooperative could understand different cultural mindsets and master social interaction. I used my past experiences as a basis to improve and build on other experiences in real-life situations. I realized that this was a cooperative of about 500 members, led by a single person, the president, who had created a hierarchy based on his personal interests like family, friends, and supporters, all to maintain his power perpetually.

Description of the Central Office

The central office can be aptly characterized as a vibrant space, animated by a multitude of workers sporting broad smiles on their lips and faces – smiles that occasionally appeared somewhat forced. The atmosphere was one of continuous greetings, where everyone acknowledged each other without any apparent reason. To me, this place felt akin to paradise. As a man raised in an African country marked by English colonization, my mindset had been moulded by a pragmatic lifestyle influenced by a fusion of Afro-American and Anglo-Saxon cultures. Here, within the cooperative's headquarters, I harboured a deep curiosity to explore the intricacies of the Latin cultural structure and its unique ability to transform everyday life into celebrations and artistic expressions.

The scene in that office triggered recollections of the impressions I had amassed over the years regarding Italian/Latin people. Initially, I noticed the pervasive presence of a network of familial connections that seemed to permeate every facet of their lives. Additionally, the influence of Catholic Christianity, symbolized, for example, by an emblem dear to the mafia, was evident, as was a cultural inclination toward peace. This was a society culturally non-violent, despite the mafia's original footprint being rooted in this very place. This locale, the birthplace of Commedia dell'Arte, reveled in heroes and the veneration of saints.

However, over time, within this nebulous reality, I began to comprehend that these exaggerated manifestations, which could be described as a form of empathy, were, in fact, indicative of psychological distress. I coined the term "psychological fatigue distress" to encapsulate this emotional and mental stress, deeply rooted in various sources of continuous stress. Many individuals in this office seemed to lack a clear reason for their presence, often contributing little or nothing to justify their existence. This recurring pattern was a carbon copy of what transpired in other projects within the organization, as I later discovered.

My insatiable curiosity impelled me to investigate the situation within the cooperative. I focused on various aspects, including the dynamics of communication, the requisite workforce, task availability, the rationale underpinning the system, activity planning, and the operational strategies of the entire setup. This investigative process was founded on my keen observation and thorough analysis of the social resources present in a cooperative.

Management Like That of a Clan

With this book, I am bringing to light what cannot remain hidden due to my interest in understanding what is happening in the context of social assistance, with a focus on solidarity. I want to specify that these are only some aspects that I am able to share for now. Often, it is thought that what remains hidden from the masses concerns national secrets or intellectual property, or matters that might clash with the cultural and legal context of a community. In the private sector, this attitude might be considered legitimate to satisfy the legal basis of intellectual property. But in the field of social solidarity, we are already in the public domain that could be considered a no man's land or as everyone's land. In the field of social solidarity, the collective and democratic approach should prevail, avoiding the accumulation of power in the hands of a few. However, in this case, we are talking about the social management of a civil society for the good of the people. Instead, things unfold completely differently within the cooperative in a secretive manner. After becoming a full-fledged member of the cooperative, I realized with surprise that the majority of the so-called worker-members in the central office had some form of connection, both familial and friendship, with the president. Those who didn't fit into these circles were constantly in conflict with him, considered almost an outcast despite their services being vital to the organization. What initially seemed like a family dynamic in the office now revealed a different agenda, and I realized that my initial perception had been influenced by my "intellectual naivety." My understanding strengthened: this approach entailed various provisions:

1) a consistent and conscious attitude, helping and allowing deep understanding without prejudice and an almost perfect ability to observe;

2) this attitude not only enhanced personality but ensured respect for/from both God and the Devil, 'ironically speaking';

3) furthermore, it helped develop greater awareness in formulating judgments in different situations;

4) Finally, this serenity always ensured a focused attention for a distinctive and privileged observation of every phenomenon.

This is what I learned from life then: behavioural consistency is a fundamental virtue for the dignity of making facts evident and forming opinions based on reality, not hearsay.

Hierarchy Within the Cooperative

When talking about this COOPERATIVE, we refer to the real protagonists who are orchestrating this somewhat unethical game. The true actors are three individuals: number 1 is the president, while the other two have alternated for years in the position of vice-president. The cooperative becomes merely a means to satisfy their illicit appetites. The president uses the other two members, assigning them key roles to achieve his goals. This trio consists of two men and a woman.

My Experience in 2016

The first case of suspicion that struck me dates back to 2016. I want to share an episode that sheds light on the nature of these people, not only as individuals but as those entrusted with managing social solidarity works for the needy within society. On one unfortunate day, a dark evening, I had an appointment with a paediatrician for a medical examination for one of the children with his mother who lived in one of the refugee accommodations managed by the cooperative. That evening, only two families were remaining to be visited by the doctor. The other family consisted of a father and a girl with some difficulties. Due to the girl's conditions, being a father myself, I felt deeply involved in their situation. At that moment, my attention was captured by the girl with a feeling of compassion. Meanwhile, however, I left my bag unattended, containing about 700 euros. Before I could realize it, that man, the girl's father, had stolen my wallet along with all the money, documents, and credit cards inside. That man wasn't a native of this place; he seemed to come from Eastern Europe, a deduction supported both by his appearance and linguistic accent. Indeed, we did introduce ourselves to each other. At this point, you might wonder why I carried so much money during working hours. In those years, working with the cooperative in the immigrant project (reception), this was my reality. I promptly reported the theft to the local police. However, the justice process that followed was strange and hurried to me, and I was informed that there was nothing the police could do. The evidence was considered insufficient to prove that the man in question had committed the theft, despite only our two families being present at the time. The handling of this episode ultimately helped me emphasize how oligarchs can manipulate and exploit false pretexts to bypass every bureaucratic tool, even when not strictly necessary. I informed the office of what happened, and it seemed that everyone was sympathetic to my situation. After some time, the then vice-president, a woman, suggested that I should file a theft report with the police to get reimbursement for the stolen amount. I then submitted the report I made to our office through the same vice-president, but in the end, the reimbursement I got was made with a different justification. This episode represented my first sign of suspicion regarding their conduct. Even though I handed over the police report to the office. In theory, there would have been nothing wrong if the reimbursement had been made with the correct justification, from my point of view. During the period when we were managing the immigrant reception project, there were always three associate workers working, often involved in taking care of about 30 refugees simultaneously. The expenses to be faced were continuous and practically daily. Despite everything, I was the only one not provided with a payment card, even though most of the daily expenses fell on me. This circumstance might also have shades of racism, but that is not the main focus of my narrative. Furthermore, I was the only one with a degree from a university in this country, but I never had a say. Nevertheless, my colleagues always relied on me, and we mutually respected each other's work. My work experience with them was undoubtedly positive. However, I found myself relegated to a subordinate role, like a simple courier, by the bosses (the oligarchs).

The Operational Role of the Cultural and Linguistic Mediator

In short, a cultural and linguistic mediator plays a crucial role within an organization dealing with immigration issues in a country. Their services are designed to facilitate communication and understanding among individuals from different cultural and linguistic backgrounds, with all the nuances that come with it. Their task is fundamental in creating an inclusive and supportive environment for all individuals, regardless of their cultural or linguistic background.

I would like to clarify first that the work of the cultural and linguistic mediator is not recognized as an integral part of the integration program by cooperatives in this country. We are considered a simple tool at their service, to be used at their discretion. My initial intention was noble when I joined the organization. Within the cooperative, the services I provided were extensive: ranging from the role of cultural and linguistic mediator to legal consultant for immigrants, responsible for the anti-trafficking program, responsible for disputes, and responsible for the transport of immigrants, just to name a few. I was always available 24 hours a day in case of emergency and yet was never compensated for availability, even though it would have been fair to do so. I considered my commitment a contribution to the good of society, an incarnation of the ideal of social solidarity. I also took care of their needs, such as food and clothing. The cooperative exploited my skills, credentials, and commitment to secure contracts, but I was regularly employed only as a driver or as an untrained social worker. My name never appeared in the official programs of the organization as the person responsible for all these tasks, except occasionally during their presentations when the issue of image was at stake for them. These responsibilities were sometimes shared with my colleagues. In the end, these responsibilities were deemed useless by the oligarchs, as their interest was focused not on the goals and results of the organization, but on what they could gain from the organization as long as they remained in their positions.

My Experiences with Organizational and Contractual Inconsistencies

On a memorable day, I attended a conference during which the exciting news of funding for an ambitious project aimed at solving a crucial issue that the country cared about was disclosed. Unfortunately, reality turned out to be very different: among the thousands of expected beneficiaries, only a few had actually benefited from this project. On the other hand, those who had obtained the contract, often based on bureaucratic requirements only on papers (lacking actual skills), seemed to have no interest in the real needs of the people involved or the society which is striving to solve a problem. It was disconcerting to note how these providers, instead of directing resources towards collective well-being, they were enjoying a life of luxury thanks to the huge profits accumulated. In other words, the system seems designed to favour those who already have power and resources while placing more obstacles for those who have less at their disposal. It is even more surprising to observe that, in this country, every initiative aimed at helping the less fortunate often ends up resulting in the creation of internal bureaucracies and the maintenance of administrative offices, with disproportionate salaries and benefits for the oligarchs. Meanwhile, those in need who should benefit from these initiatives are often left behind with little or nothing. This paradoxical scenario seems to perpetuate the dependence of the less fortunate on those who should be serving a higher cause, thus perpetuating a cycle of exploitation. My experiences in the field of social work have led me to an important revelation, which I have learned over time: I noticed that when profit depends on the number of disadvantaged individuals or patients involved in projects by funding the private sector with supported public funds, there is always the risk of favouring personal enrichment; The fear of losing a job or contract becomes an obstacle to providing high-quality services, pushing the monetary aspect of the said project to the forefront of a person's attention; Bureaucracy within a democratic system can often become overexposed and hinder people with fewer opportunities, making their already disadvantaged situation due to poverty, illness, and other hardships even more difficult; In other words, the system seems to privilege those who are already powerful and resourceful, while making the road harder for those who have less at their disposal.

Personal Experience in a Senseless Project

Needy people often find themselves deprived of their rights due to costly bureaucratic challenges in filing a complaint, creating perpetual dependence and constant exploitation in favour of the oligarchs. This results in an endless cycle where the less fortunate are forced into silence or submission because any other option is simply too costly in terms of time and knowledge. Moreover, there is no guarantee that they will get the attention they deserve; on the contrary, the action could further worsen their situation. I directly participated in an initiative where funds were allocated to help struggling families. This project, contracted to the cooperative by the municipality, actually required an expenditure of 100 euros but cost 750 euros monthly for each assistance. This example shows how vulnerable people are exploited and deceived by those who have power and control. I believe that such a project would have had greater value and been more effective if it had been managed directly by the municipality's social services, to directly benefit the people involved rather than outsourcing it to third parties. "I think this redundancy and superfluous connections were deliberate to bureaucratically facilitate the intent of corruption." I have had various experiences in different working contexts that I could share to offer a more in-depth understanding of the complexity of these situations of structural impediment. However, my ability to communicate is limited by the arduous literary effort required to describe every detail exhaustively.

Incompetent Maintenance Officer

Every project coordinator acts like a feudal lord, operating in a kind of medieval kingdom marked by neglect. This management style has resulted in a significant waste of human and financial resources within the cooperative, a stark incongruity in modern times. On several occasions, I observed resources of all kinds being squandered without any control. For instance, a person assigned to the maintenance role, favoured by the oligarchies due to his subservience, lacked the necessary skills. His primary task was to provide them with information about those opposing their interests. This maintenance officer often made trips of over 50 km, consuming time and resources, perhaps just to change a single light bulb in one of the cooperative's houses. Every time I exchanged the cooperative's vehicles for work with him, I always found an assortment of unused materials in the vehicles, demonstrating recklessness but convenient expenses for his personal interests and usage for his personal affairs, thanks to his freedom in using the cooperative's funds.

Unjust Dismissal for the Common Good: Meetings and Social Deception

A tangible example of injustice manifests itself through the dismissal of one of the most passionate employees of a cooperative. This person had developed a deep understanding of the project she was involved in, thanks to her dedication and passion. Her knowledge had reached a point where she became a fundamental resource, but her dismissal led to the irreparable loss of this valuable know-how. This type of attitude can also be found in the way our cooperative discontinued our project for progressive purposes. Meetings involving power and positions of influence are mainly reserved for the president or for those he has chosen, without considering their skills or the value they could have added to the improvements of the necessary resources. In this way, associate workers (members) are forced to firmly align even more with the centre of procedures and administrative power for their employment security, "because what has never been done often creates fear" (a systematic distancing of others from the management centre), and they know it. I still remember when we were going around holding meetings together with other cooperatives in various places to discuss what was needed to be done to improve the management system of immigration reception in this country. It was quite amusing to see that, as it was also happening in most other cooperatives, we were always represented by those workers who didn't even know what was needed to be done or by those who didn't want to end up on the president's blacklist but were selected by the various presidents themselves. These representatives attending these meetings without being able to contribute anything to the meeting but only to take notes and report information back to the office for the decisions of the oligarchy, knowing nothing, for example, about immigration. The system seems sick, as personal interest takes on a predominant role, generating further problems. In the meetings, participation in the discussions was often reserved for a few individuals, while others were excluded from the debate, contributing to creating an environment adverse to collective involvement. A personal example of this dynamic was during one of the few meetings I had the opportunity to attend.

During my participation in a discussion on a subject in which I had expertise, the moderator abruptly inquired about my identity in a rather impolite manner. Furthermore, in another course I also attended, the instructor repeatedly interrupted me, alleging that I was monopolizing the discussion by sharing information, even though we were practicing a group exercise. This information, however, could have been valuable for those who were relatively new to the subject and would benefit from additional insights for further reflection on the topic at hand. In that context, I was sharing my personal experiences with others to provide a broader perspective on the issues at hand. Being the only one with extensive cultural experience, even temporally and realistically, I found it important to share my opinions to contribute to the resolution of the disputes. These experiences denote a structural problem that limits the sharing of knowledge for the benefit of the community.

The Unjust Delegation of Social Issues to Cooperatives Rather Than Public Administration

Today, the cooperative has become the focal point of a complex social deception. Most cooperatives seem to have deliberately taken positions that reflect a system that tolerates human abuses. In this way, the cooperative is also believed to be the only entity capable of addressing the situation for its long-term association with social issues of their respective communities. This attitude might be the result of a careful analysis of how the current system allows such abuses, but at the same time, it could also represent a form of intentional complexity that rejects the action of public administration. Thus arises a complex and problematic situation, suggesting that only the cooperative falsely possesses the means to address it. Disproportionate bureaucratic formulations by the Central

Government in the sector could be the result of continuous funding requests from cooperatives. At the same time, there is a lack of suggestions from cooperatives for the implementation of innovative strategies that would reduce expenses sustainably. This could indicate a systematic willingness of cooperatives to distance public administration from social issues, letting the State try to address fraud through increasingly bureaucratic legislation. In conclusion, the delegation of social issues to cooperatives seems to be a way to keep the State away from solving such problems, due to a lack of understanding of how to proceed. This intrinsic complexity leads to a deceptive cycle that perpetuates a system that could be more effectively managed by public administration.

Management of Hospitality: A Reflection on Culture and Social Deception

Within this specific hospitality project, I pose a question: have those involved in cooperatives seriously examined the meaning of the word 'culture,' particularly the concept of a "cultural mediator"? Despite the presence of sociologists, psychologists, anthropologists, and similar figures who are adept at being rhetorically outspoken about these issues in public, the reality is that their understanding and awareness of these same issues may differ, and it seems that this aspect is often overlooked. In practice, there might be a disparity between their public discourse and their personal perspectives on these matters.

In my previous commitment, I sought to structurally define an authentic form of interaction and mutual aid within the concept of 'hospitality.' This effort aimed to provide a model for future use, a guide that could help anyone new to the field. In other words, I tried to promote a project of sustainable inclusion by involving my colleagues. Despite joint efforts with other project operators, the decision-making powers of the oligarchies within the cooperative often hindered the formulation of authentic and sustainable hospitality that embraced true social reintegration. Instead, immigrants were often seen as a way to generate profits, with little attention to their social needs and an agenda driven by an attitude of paternalism rather than inclusion. Every time I tried to bring this issue to their attention, I was ignored or treated with disdain. It seemed that my proposal was considered bothersome.

I firmly believe that collective experience and current education are essential to address future challenges, especially in the social field, as they involve lives and tangible realities.

The Figure of the President: Autocracy and Abuse of Power

The president, a central figure within this cooperative, seems to wield excessive power and uses it to pursue personal interests. Meetings with the oligarchies governing the cooperative appear to serve only as a pretext, a way to divert attention from autocratic decisions. This system is designed to obscure transparency and muddy the waters, turning the Board of Directors (CDA) bureaucratically into a means to justify the president's actions. The president uses the organization's financial strength to oppress or eliminate any member of the organization who tries to be an obstacle on his path to personal gain. The president's luxury car, purchased with cooperative funds, and almost of all their vices are funded by the same cooperative. These are just a few examples of how the financial system is abused for personal gain. The other vice-presidents seem to enjoy similar privileges, and all seem to consider themselves above the statutory rules in a veiled manner. The president became president before I joined the organization about 7 years ago, long before writing this book. The president seems to have the desire to maintain this position in the long term, directing the cooperative's resources towards his personal interest without caring about the cooperative's future. This excessive and autocratic ambition can have a devastating impact on the community, with the needs of the less fortunate being sacrificed for personal gain. Moreover, the perpetual dependence and lack of improvement in the conditions of project beneficiaries raise questions about the cooperative's true intention. People should be at the centre of attention, but it seems that money has taken precedence, leading to a range of ethical and social problems. In conclusion, it is crucial to rethink how these projects are managed, focusing on beneficiaries and inclusion. The whole context leaves me perplexed, especially given that I am not an expert in psychology (although I have developed a basic understanding through lived experiences and personal insights), yet I have been able to contribute successfully in various cases involving psychological and psychiatric issues encountered among immigrants during my work with them. It is essential to emphasize that I could do so thanks to the collaboration of public hospitals and the support of true industry experts. That said, I wonder: why do the vast majority of patients who join the cooperative program seem doomed to depend on medications and be housed long-term? This dependency seems to turn into a kind of perpetual imprisonment, raising important questions. Yet, I have an answer that I can offer sincerely: it seems to be exclusively about "money, without any consideration for the unfortunate lives involved or for the well-being of society or all of humanity." It's as if cooperatives, in the name of the disadvantaged, their only interest has become financial profit. This state of affairs should change so that the primary goal is no longer the wealth accumulated at the expense of the less fortunate but instead the well-being and progress of all. It's time for cooperatives to end this reckless race for money and focus instead on a true commitment to healing, independence, and improving the lives of those seeking help. I repeat: the cooperative should stop exploiting the needs of the less fortunate for its own gain and instead focus on genuine social commitment. Only then can we hope for a fairer and more compassionate society where authentic cooperation surpasses the blind pursuit of financial gain.

Anti-Solidarity Episodes: Reflections on Society and Deception

A question of reflection arises: what purpose does a welfare system serve in a democratic society? The concept of welfare should ensure assistance and well-being for citizens. The interconnection between welfare and democracy requires the responsible participation of all citizens, creating a synergy that should lead to collective well-being and happiness. However, in today's societies, challenges related to disability, poverty, illness, detention, misfortune, and similar circumstances have become oppressive to bear. These difficulties not only affect those directly involved but also impose a considerable burden on their families. For them, these situations often represent a life sentence, while most of society remains distant from such realities, grasping them only superficially through the media. However, there is ample evidence that demonstrates how these situations are exploited for personal gain by cooperatives. Often, when funds are requested from the government or other organizations on behalf of the needy, these funds are redirected to the cooperatives' elites. A glaring example of this phenomenon is evident in numerous advertising campaigns created to support the less fortunate. However, the funds collected do not always reach those in need, instead swelling the pockets of cooperative elites. Consider clothing bins or banners left in neighbourhoods on behalf of the needy. Even training courses entrusted to cooperatives sometimes generate profits rather than promoting social assistance. This attitude destroys the trust of people who donate items or resources in good faith, seeing them exploited for profit.

Management of Activities for Community Guests

I vividly recall numerous meetings cantered around the administration of services for guests within our mental health facilities. To this day, I am disturbed by certain managerial assertions suggesting a lack of concern for individuals attending school or engaging in recreational activities, particularly when guests are under the influence of psychotropic substances. This mindset is unacceptable, reflecting an approach that prioritizes cutting project costs over enhancing the lives of those involved. In the past, I came across an intriguing master's program at the University of Padua. Expressing interest, I sought permission from cooperative leaders to participate and take a few days off, but my request was unequivocally denied. Their focus appears solely on my precarious employment, neglecting any improvement in my contribution to the overall project setup. Subsequently, I discovered that two members of the same group were enrolled in educational programs—one, the female vice president, pursuing a master's degree, and the other serving as a pawn to complete a bachelor's degree. This revelation raised suspicions of deceptive practices.

Suspected False Statements: The Unveiled Deception

On a routine day, I accompanied our new accountant to a public office. This individual was hired after three accountants cycled through, seemingly in pursuit of someone willing to align with their dubious plans. He appeared to fit the bill—a young, easily manipulated person with aspirations for power and conveniently connected as the brother-in-law of a staunch supporter. They couldn't avoid having me accompany him due to my colleagues being unavailable. This marks the beginning of a tale involving misleading and suspicious financial statements.

While perusing the financial statements presented to the office, I observed expenses that seemed implausible for our project. Unfortunately, my curiosity was hampered by the lack of verification opportunities, as the mentioned services were never executed in our cooperative project. Encountering such questionable financial statements in public offices became a growing concern. The statements featured expenses and service titles unrelated to our immigrant hospitality project, and funds appeared to vanish into obscure channels, diverting valuable resources from the cooperative to personal coffers. When complaints about the financial situation arose, I grasped the reality of the situation—the workers would eventually be held accountable for dishonest behaviour and systematic theft from the cooperative. The documentation presented for signatures or approvals often seemed one-sided during assemblies. We were compelled to give consent without access to checks, driven by the fact that our survival depended on the cooperative. Despite our dissatisfaction, protests remained clandestine. The cooperative's resources seemed concentrated in the hands of three individuals. To benefit, one had to align with them, become their personal puppet, and pursue their goals, often at the expense of social solidarity. This situation becomes more problematic considering that the Board of Directors (CDA) exists only on paper, emphasizing bureaucracy over real accountability. Some accepted these conditions, sacrificing ethics, human dignity, and even spiritual beliefs. Those who resisted often faced negative consequences. Only corrupt leaders had the authority to approve cooperative expenses, which included allocations to third parties or individuals considered "staunch supporters." Their financial decisions extended to organizing events, parties, dinners, and gift distributions, all aimed at cultivating and preserving their personal image. Paradoxically, this practice is justified as a strategy promoting the cooperative's overall interests. I reiterate: the situation is further complicated by the fact that the Board of Directors (CDA) exists only on paper, prioritizing bureaucracy over genuine accountability.

Exploitation of Workers: An Alarming System

My experience as a driver for this cooperative has been more than disappointing. Every day, I was tasked with delivering food and materials to various locations indiscriminately, often unrealistically and in distant places, considering traffic and logistical conditions. To meet tight delivery deadlines, I ended up violating traffic laws and regulations. Once, cameras captured my reckless behaviour, and I had to pay a fine out of my pocket according to cooperative policies. If Amazon is often criticized for its unfair practices towards couriers, it is equally important to draw attention to the cooperative I worked for. The latter, along with others like it, has demonstrated an even worse approach in terms of operations and treatment of its drivers. Take my case as an example: when I worked on the immigrant's hospitality project, I was not paid adequately according to a regular contract, as happened in some other cooperatives. Despite my 24/7 commitment, even during leave, my hours were not considered. In this cooperative, many workers are underpaid; some even receive less than the hours worked, while others are forced to work for free or in secret for the elites. Doesn't this phenomenon represent a modern form of "caporalato"? During the COVID-19 epidemic, we had to face unsafe working conditions. Especially in nursing homes, adequate protective devices were lacking. Anyone daring to raise a criticism was considered a traitor rather than an ally in facing a crisis. This culture of silence prevented effective management of the situation, jeopardizing everyone's health. Worker safety should be a corporate priority, but it seems that this concept is often sacrificed for profit.

The Ignored Proposals in Favour of Cooperation

I came forward with a proposal that I believed could contribute to solving the immigration problem in this country in a unique way. My colleagues welcomed the proposal with enthusiasm, but the so-called leaders proved to be timid and sceptical about it. They were not in favour of cohesion among the associated workers in the immigrant section within the cooperative. The idea of seeing us work together in peace bothered them, fearing that it threatened their position. They were more inclined to embrace an outdated philosophy that propagated division as a means to gain or maintain power.

However, the problem extended to the operation of the immigrant section within the cooperative itself. Despite being one of the most profitable projects, if not the most profitable, it was paradoxically kept in the shadows. It was unique, a project without deliberate flaws, geared towards improving skills and constant development. But why was it being kept hidden? To this day, this question remains unanswered.

Internal Conflicts: The Struggle for Balance

Issues with the so-called "masters" (the oligarchs of the cooperative) have always been on the agenda, especially when it came to providing services for the community. Their personal interests often clashed with the vision of society. The discrepancy between these perspectives caused friction and made it difficult to deliver efficient services. Despite the challenges, we tried to maintain a balanced commitment, considering both the well-being of the community and the needs of the cooperative. Our mission has always been to create social value and well-being, respecting the rights of all and maintaining a relationship of trust between the two perspectives.

Paths of Change: From Outdated Ideology to Progress

The strategy and planning of the "masters" often relied on the idea of "it has always been done this way, so we will continue to do it." This outdated mentality left little room for innovation and community improvement. Instead of investing in a thorough analysis of the situation, we need to adopt a progressive and sustainable approach to meet current needs. We must build a relationship based on rational assessments and not on outdated ideologies. This is crucial to creating effective and harmonious human coexistence.

For me, one of humanity's most significant intellectual advancements is our ability to engage in rational reasoning. This skill should guide our choices, especially when dealing with complex social issues.

The "Salvini Reform" of Immigrant's Hospitality: Analysis and Reflections

Recently, I pondered the cooperative's contribution to addressing the immigration problem, beyond responding to budget measures and reforms by the relevant Minister. The "Salvini Reform" regarding immigrants, part of the so-called "Salvini Decree on Immigration and Security" approved in September 2018, addressed the issue decisively, albeit not exhaustively and somewhat confusedly due to the lack of a fundamental structural formulation regarding the current reality of the situation. While it could be improved, it represented a step forward in addressing a thorny social problem. However, the lack of collaboration from those who should have supported the initiative made its success challenging. This problem is a symptom of an already chaotic situation where national interests should prevail over political considerations (why was his party left alone to face the problem, ultimately favouring the oligarchy). The Minister was correct about the excessive funds allocated to the program, which was also accompanied by redundant bureaucracy. The reform lays the groundwork for modernizing immigrant's hospitality in Italy. This topic will be further explored by me at an opportune time in a future analysis of sustainable immigration regulation. In conclusion, the path to sustainable change requires a rational approach and constant commitment for the good of society. If leadership is lacking, the entire system will suffer, just like a body without a head guiding its actions.

Considerations on Political Sympathy and Approach to Social Justice

Although I do not identify with the positions of the political Right, I am convinced that justice must always be recognized for our common good. Civil society is based on the foundation of social justice as a fundamental principle. My observations on the social world and its laws are based on solid intellectual foundations, aiming to be consistent with the reality we live in. This implies that the social principles I follow are guided by rational evaluation, without being influenced by ideologies, political colours, or ethnic differences. We must constantly remind ourselves that humanity is at the centre of our circumstances, and everything around us is part of its reality. However, I digress from the main topic for a moment.

The Rise to Power of the 5 Star Movement and the Northern League

When the 5 Star Movement and the Northern League came to power in Italy on June 1, 2018, with Matteo Salvini as the Minister of internal affairs, there was a stir of interest among the cooperative oligarchs and beneficiaries of the system. This reform had been requested several times during the electoral campaign by the League. This period revealed how influential cooperative oligarchs were thanks to their lobbying skills. It should be noted, however, that until the beginning of this account, there had been no real change in terms of the reform, especially regarding the funding of the 'immigrant's hospitality project.' This underscores the fact that the poor and needy can be considered sources of profit for the true owners of cooperatives, who are sometimes far from the idea of social solidarity. The reform might have been adopted on paper, but its implementation was hindered by the influence of the oligarchs. A closer look would have revealed that the main problem was not only the lives of immigrants or the country's difficulties in handling the situation but also the financial reform of the institutions involved in immigration.

The Closure and Resumption of the Immigration Project

When the hospitality reform was promulgated on September 24, 2018, our cooperative decided to close the immigration project, even though there was no financial deficit with the new decree. However, when the opportunity arose to make huge profits from the unfortunate tragedy in Ukraine, the cooperative decided to resume activity, but only for cynical profit reasons and not for humanitarian reasons. Our only problem was that we were losing the convenience of earning abundant profits.

Brief Reflections on Immigration

Immigration can have value only if it is sustainable. I am not only considering the superficial aspect, such as the need for athletes or non-specialized workers, which are the most celebrated types of immigrants in Italy. Cultural updating is essential, including the acquisition of technical, political, and social skills, along with a cultural orientation enriched with distinct values. This should go beyond solidarity. Furthermore, a comprehensive reform is needed both top-down and bottom-up to create a stable and powerful society that embraces evolution and innovation.

Investigation into the Dysfunction of the Cooperative System and My Growing Awareness

The beginning of my research to understand the situation within the cooperative system and its malfunctioning was driven by my observation of the incongruence between reality and the objectives of the cooperative oligarchs. In order to be more humanly and culturally aware and confident about what was happening, to understand the case and to be able to tell the facts factually and visibly. This questionable attitude prompted me to delve into the situation, opening my eyes beyond superficial appearances. I undertook this research with the goal of becoming more aware and informed about the situation so that I could tell the facts clearly and objectively. I shared my concerns with my colleagues to have an open discussion about the situation. Many of them recognized the corruption within the cooperative system. Some even decided to leave their jobs to avoid further problems.

It is interesting to note that sometimes people decide to leave not only to seek better job opportunities but because of the humiliation they have to endure at work. In fact, I noticed that when it comes to Italians leaving their jobs, it is not necessarily an attitude of seeking better employment, but often it is due to the humiliation they have to endure at work. Others decide to stay for their personal interests, not so much for those of the cooperative, with the attitude of "I don't care." However, none of them was ready to join me in trying to figure out what could be done to improve things.

In our cooperative, there are people who tend to have a frivolous attitude towards our vehicles, often exchanging them quickly to meet their convenience or leisure needs. Sometimes they can change up to four vehicles in a single day, while others are forced to use their own cars for cooperative tasks. However, this trend has a significant impact on the costs we had to face, including for fuels, insurances, maintenance, materials, reimbursements, and so on. In addition to the evident waste of material, temporal, and human resources.

There was a more responsible and rational option, which would have consisted of appointing one of our cooperative's logistics experts to oversee the maintenance of our vehicles, but this was not done. In this way, the purchase of unnecessary new vehicles could have been avoided, reducing associated costs and promoting a culture of respect and shared responsibility for available resources.

The lack of effective communication was one of the factors that contributed to this situation. The oligarchs preferred those who were ready to say "yes, sir," rather than genuinely involved collaborators. This attitude led to a dysfunctional work environment and hindered real reflection on social solidarity. Thus, even those chosen benefited from the cooperative, albeit to a lesser extent. This was the first time I worked with such a terrible group of intellectuals ignorant of the value of "collectivity," equipped only with superficial egocentrism.

I tried to raise issues with the leaders as a collaborator and member of the cooperative in the hope of reflecting on the issue of social solidarity, but my rationality was misunderstood, and my relationship with them deteriorated. Additionally, I noticed partial treatment from the leaders. When the issues concerned my colleagues, the solutions were often punitive rather than corrective. Instead, when they themselves were involved, they often completely ignored the situation. This lack of clarity and coherence is a sign of a malfunctioning system. I tried to address the oligarchs, but my attempt was rejected, and I began to understand their selfishness and lack of interest in the common good. This kind of partial and different treatment depending on the people is not the right way to address the legitimate problems of the associated workers (members) according to our cooperative agreement. Sometimes, I managed to meet one of the leaders in the offices during working hours after many futile efforts, only to discuss the efficiency of our services and the possibility of sustaining the costs ourselves. The absence of an effective communication method and the lack of respect for cooperative principles led to a waste of material and human resources. I suggested that a logistics expert oversee the maintenance of the vehicles, but this option was not considered, leading to excessive costs and waste. However, I was never thinking that the situation was as always worse like this.

In the past, I was thinking that there was the willingness to work together, but over time I was able to understand that there was no collaboration at all. The lack of communication favoured division within the group. I found myself having to confront the oligarchs, but I realized that my approach was not welcome. Because they only listened to me in passing, putting pressure on me only if our interaction could be useful to their personal interests, not our common interest. This became the only way to talk to them, as coordinators were not authorized to make decisions, not even the simplest ones.

Every time we faced disputes in the workplace, instead of inviting both parties involved to resolve the issue, they will turn the disagreement into gossip in order to favour a division strategy within the group for their benefit. I remember that one day I had the opportunity to speak to the three oligarchs about this serious situation in the cooperative. We came to the point of discussing why not fire people without valid justification, instead of always trying to reach an agreement before excluding them from the cooperative: if they had legitimate reasons? I asked them this question when they always tried to blame others for the embarrassing situation of the cooperative, but I didn't receive a convincing answer. For this above-mentioned reason, I decided to confront the oligarchs by expressing that it was not the best way to treat members who work in solidarity and collaboration. I was told that they didn't have to act according to my expectations, which was also diplomatically correct as a response but was, in reality, in another way round the intention behind the response was devilish and cunning. For me, that attitude was cynical and selfish and did not solve our collective problem: because the reality on the ground justifies the current situation! My observation was seen as a threat by them. At this point, I began to understand their game, and they also started keeping an eye on me.

I wondered continually if it was possible to build over time a work and cooperation ethic in a rational way, beyond a useless cult of antisocial solidarity? The confusion for no reason within the core of the system lacks concrete elements, a sense of cooperative norm, and civil discipline, favouring widespread incompetence with no evidence of resource efficiency and sustainability. This situation has also led to reluctant communication among the associated workers, united only by superficial chatter without a real exchange of social value. I began to understand that the system was cantered on personal interests rather than social solidarity. The inability to build a work and cooperation ethic has led to general inefficiency. Communication among workers was limited and superficial. In conclusion, here we find ourselves facing something resembling isolated feudalism in today's irrational world, created only for personal interests, just like back then! It is essential to address this situation and seek a sustainable solution to promote real and responsible cooperation.

A Change of Role and the Discovery of Dubious Engagements

The change of role I experienced was a moment of great challenge and revelation. Understanding various aspects of our expenses, I had ample evidence to show that we were spending much less than the government fund allocation recently disclosed by the Ministry of Salvini. While attempting to prevent the closure of the immigration project, I realized that the so-called leaders already had their plans in mind, without directly involving us. Despite my efforts to make them reason and consider the consequences, the project was closed. This made me reflect on the competence of the leaders and their desire to preserve their financial security at the expense of assigned responsibilities. This behaviour can lead to the misuse of funds and irrational decisions. It was a moment of great disappointment, as I realized I was not considered a true partner but merely an executor. This situation taught me that when someone is incompetent in their assigned job, they tend to prioritize their personal financial security over fulfilling their responsibilities. This can lead to the misuse of funds to their advantage. In fact, they already had their plans on what to do, and these plans were kept secret from us project operators. None of the associated workers was truly considered their partner, as it should be. This was one of the saddest moments of my life, filled with great disappointment. I decided that perhaps it was the right time for me to leave the cooperative after all that I had been through.

Due to my curiosity to delve into the cause of what was happening, I decided to wait and see what their other goal was to replace the immigrant program. Because they had decided to close it without involving us project operators directly interested. It was also at that moment that the COVID-19 pandemic broke out, making this period even more complex, but it was also a time of learning and growth. I decided to stay in the cooperative to see what their new alternative project would be, involving the three of us who were once managing the immigrant's hospitality project. The decision to stay in this cooperative has been one of the most fruitful decisions I have ever made since working with them. After some time in my new role as a driver, I learned to understand that "the darkest hour of the night is also the hour closest to dawn." In this narrative, I am only scratching the surface of the entire problem we were going through day by day. I have heard and seen much more than I can testify to on how I experienced this soulless and materialistic situation.

My New Experience as a Driver

My new experience as a driver has opened my eyes to the reality of this cooperative. We have various branches in different municipalities and manage a wide range of facilities, including nursing homes, psychiatric facilities, nurseries, and catering services, as well as assistance personnel associated with different municipalities, in addition to some sports complexes, etc. I thought I had seen enough of their antisocial behaviour to confirm their dubious activities, but my change of role has allowed me to learn more about their reality, facts I had only heard about before. This made me realize how extensive the activities of the cooperative were and how necessary effective coordination was. I began to wonder why there were so many drivers. The composition of the group seemed to be based on personal relationships rather than skills. This made me reflect on the lack of structural efficiency and human resource management. I tried to suggest improvements, but I was hindered by the egocentric attitude of the oligarchs.

As a Driver

In this new role of mine, there were four drivers. I couldn't understand why we needed to be so many. This was my thought as I observed how each of us had been hired:

1) One of us was the godfather of the president's son, who was employed with a higher job grade;

2) Our coordinator also had her transportation company, which was in direct competition with our cooperative;

3) There was another man from the south working part-time;

4) And then there was me, the only graduate, but also one of the lowest-paid along with the man from the south.

In short, there wasn't enough work for all of us, which certainly demonstrated their lack of structural efficiency. They lacked personnel and the skills each of us possessed for other activities within the cooperative. I made several efforts to discuss how we could better organize ourselves and improve our services to attract more value both internally and externally, involving everyone in different entities and qualities of participation. However, their egocentric and irrational attitude prevented us from embarking on an innovative path together.

After some of the initial meetings we had after my entry into this new role, the oligarchs once again indicated that my intention had not changed even a bit and that my attitude could jeopardize their strategy. From that moment, they started avoiding me. Due to my constant effort to find a reasonable way of working together that could also prevent potential contract losses due to the entire system back then, they began doing everything to distance me from the cooperative. They assigned me fewer tasks and continually reduced my working hours, putting me under constant pressure. This was the same strategy they had always used to exclude anyone from the cooperative who was not subject to their direct manipulation.

My Unsettling Personality and the Struggle for Change

Once, a Neapolitan colleague told me, "Prince, haven't you realized that we are not paid to think here?" This comment was directed at me when I was constantly trying to contribute to the improvement of our collaboration despite the lack of proper leadership. Some colleagues wondered why I didn't just mind my own business. I always responded that I wasn't there solely to pursue my personal interests but to contribute to the building of a stronger, more inclusive community and, above all, to create a communal refuge for everyone. I believe that every action we take has an impact on the collective reality and the environment in which we live.

Furthermore, I emphasized that I would never allow the actions and attitudes of others contrary to democratic consensus to influence my aspirations. My goal is to create a model of collaboration and continuous improvement within the community where I live, here and now: a rule of law based on universal principles with their dynamics and constant development.

Collusion System - Between the Cooperative and Some Public Officials

This was my way of discovering the facts first-hand. In my opinion, there is a kind of collusion for convenience between the cooperative and some public officials, and there were situations where conflicts of interest were evident. This made me reflect on the transparency of operations and the need for greater supervision. My determination to seek change and improve the cooperative led to my isolation by the oligarchs. They assigned me fewer tasks and reduced my working hours. This exclusion strategy had been applied in the past to others and was now used on me. In conclusion, my change of role was a moment of personal growth and discovery. I witnessed the internal problems of the cooperative up close and tried to bring about improvements. However, I faced resistance from the oligarchs who preferred to maintain their control. My experience motivated me to continue seeking social justice and working for positive change.

Interaction with Colleagues and Their Dilemma

My interaction with colleagues led me to observe an interesting dynamic. As a driver, I had the opportunity to interact with associated workers in all sectors. I had the chance to conduct an objective analysis of the situation with a large margin of fairness. In all these interactions, I never found anyone who left this cooperative without considering it preferable to seek alternative employment or be unemployed rather than remain in the psychological situation they were in before quitting. This situation created a psychologically damaging atmosphere for many, so much so that some former colleagues revealed that leaving the cooperative had a positive impact on their mental health, relieving the depression and stress they had experienced working with us.

This reflection is not only about power and money but the misleading concept underlying the widespread thinking of what the cooperative should represent for "social solidarity." In short, all of this questions the concept of "social solidarity," which should be at the heart of the cooperative. My experience has shown that power and money often overshadow this noble goal.

Use of Annual Meetings Only for Personal Glorification

One of the situations I noticed is the use of annual meetings of the cooperative. Initially conceived as moments for discussing social and economic issues, they often turned into occasions for self-celebration and a moment of leisure and distraction from the cooperative's own work reality. The oligarchs took advantage of these occasions to emphasize their indispensable role as leaders of the cooperative's crew. *This too closely resembled the control tactics of the "real socialism" that was the evil of the same (single leader, control, authoritarianism, absence of plurality, lack of expression and opposition, characterized by centralized and authoritative power).* This attitude was also visible in meeting management, where limited time combined with our work commitments were used as a pretext to impose the decisions of the oligarchs. This created a climate of scepticism among the associated workers, who lost trust in real change. Year after year, the oligarchs seemed to triumph, confirming their control.

Despite the difficulties and frustrations, I continued to question and seek solutions. I was driven by a motivational and cultural desire to fully understand this phenomenon. I wanted to expose the underlying causes and find ways to counteract illicit cooperation. Thanks to this constant search, I managed to develop a greater awareness of the issues related to illicit cooperation and find new strategies to counteract it, such as the opportunity to collaborate among various professionals and participate in innovative projects aimed at promoting transparency and ethics in social economy. I believe that this constant commitment has allowed me to grow both as an individual and as a professional and be a positive contribution to the society I belong to. Additionally, I have identified the elements that hindered progress, particularly emphasizing the crucial role of incompetence in compromising any rational effort for social improvement. The choice of unqualified individuals for positions of power is a tangible threat to the well-being of a community and its sustainable growth.

The Trend of Shifting Responsibilities and Blame: A Critical Analysis

Over time, I have observed that as the oligarchies centralized power in their hands, the operational base became isolated. This situation led associated workers to become aware of illicit practices perpetrated by the top management. However, this awareness generated a sense of demoralization, where the good intentions of the workers were stifled by a feeling of powerlessness. This situation caused a distortion of priorities, with workers beginning to pursue their individual interests at the expense of cooperative goals. The original concept of social solidarity gradually faded, giving way to an atmosphere of distrust and exploited opportunities. Those who should have benefited from our services inadvertently became victims of this situation, as attention shifted from their needs to internal power games. This vicious cycle created an environment where there was always a price to pay for all involved parties. I acknowledge that the services we provide are often ineffective, and this inefficiency has become increasingly evident over time. Unfortunately, the blame seems to fall mainly on the frontline workers, those managing field projects, or taking care of the guests.

In contrast to this trend, organizational executives often evade any form of accountability, notwithstanding the mistakes that have led to service shortcomings. These errors primarily stem from their poor administrative skills and the diversion of resources from the organization itself. These aspects have been extensively documented in various parts of my writing, including false statements, indiscriminate use of gifts, and unnecessary expenses.

While my observations may be subjective, one thing is certain: I share these reflections with the community to encourage a reconsideration of the current system. It is essential to implement meaningful reforms in the cooperative structure to ensure greater transparency, accountability, and representation of the interests of the associated workers and those in need.

Initially, I had high hopes for the contribution I could make through my work within the cooperative. I wanted to play my part in bringing about significant societal change and hoped that the cooperative shared this commitment as a structure of social solidarity. However, I noticed various problems and internal challenges within the cooperative that prompted me to reflect on issues related to improving the current conditions of frontline workers and those in need.

Life is an enigma, often taken for granted, and sometimes we tend to avoid the reality of facts by consciously blaming others, temporarily suspending a deeper and logical understanding of existence.

Human behaviour often exhibits a particular tendency to shift blame onto other people or external factors while simultaneously trying to absolve oneself of actual responsibility and the ensuing consequences. For example, this dynamic is reflected in how we often attribute the responsibility for our problems to politicians when, in reality, we ourselves are often the architects of the situations we face.

This is my personal experience, and I do not intend to teach anyone sociology or political science in terms of cultural supremacy over our participation in our involvement in existence in every environment we find ourselves in. I am simply reflecting on culturally sustainable real-life nature to which we belong, driving our participation in society and the surrounding environment.

In conclusion, it is important for both the cooperative in its role and society as a whole to commit to ensuring that social workers and those in need have the opportunity to leverage their resources and be actively and adequately represented, in my opinion. As I mentioned before, my initial goal was to contribute to the best of my abilities, hoping that my society could equally contribute to improving my life mutually. The focus on the well-being of the beneficiaries has always been my priority, as they needed my help more than I needed theirs in this particular context.

"The Suffering Awaits Some of Us as We Grow Old"
A Reflection on Injustices Against the Elderly: An Apparently Venial Sin

The elderly, often voiceless and fragile, sometimes suffering from various disabilities or alone without family, are a vulnerable part of society. Here lies the crux of the problem: when these fragile individuals fall under the control of cynical individuals, their lives can turn into hell until the end of their days.

My experience as a driver serving the elderly in this cooperative has enlightened me about our vulnerability as we age. This vulnerability becomes even more apparent in precarious situations, such as poor health, lack of financial resources, and social differences. However, it is this very awareness that should guide our culture and inspire a tangible demonstration of social solidarity in our society. Only through such efforts can we build a democratic, respectful, and sustainable society that upholds human rights and honours the elderly.

Furthermore, it is essential that each of us contributes to developing this social culture and tangibly demonstrates our commitment to solidarity. We must work together to create a more inclusive and welcoming society, paying particular attention to the elderly, i.e., vulnerable people who often risk being marginalized by the system.

After the experience in which I could see how the elderly are treated, I am very afraid of aging and finding myself in their situation.

My Experience with the Elderly and Families

During my work with the elderly and disabled in this cooperative, I found a way to build good relationships with most of the families involved. My experiences with the elderly, the disabled in our cooperative, and their families have revealed a variety of reactions. I found a way to build good relationships and tried to engage the families involved. There have been several occasions when I tried to ask for help from the families of these needy people to improve the situation we were facing, to do something on their behalf, but the responses were mixed.

These were some of the contrasting responses I received:

1) Some families were concerned and eager to help their loved ones but often felt powerless in the face of a complex situation. Some preferred to further engage to avoid reporting the situation to the relevant authority.

2) Other families were indifferent, hoping that their loved ones would die soon to free themselves from a burden that afflicted them. This sense of anticipated relief was disconcerting.

3) Those who tried to protest or complain were ignored or criticized and considered annoying or a nuisance by the Cooperative.

In the end, it is evident that in this society, it is often more convenient to tolerate injustices rather than fight for one's human rights: because winning a legal battle against those who are somehow connected to power is often impossible. As a result, family members prefer not to risk losing assistance for their loved ones, even if minimal, which is always better than nothing. The injustice suffered by these elderly individuals becomes a lesser evil compared to the daily challenges they must face.

My experience has opened my eyes to the situation of the elderly and made me fear the idea of aging and finding myself in a similar position. Additionally, I have found that many operators working in the field of assisting those in need have valuable resources to share, but they are often not utilized due to the lack of incentives and adequate support, both in terms of salary and material. To promote cooperation and efficiency, these professionals need transparent support and well-deserved recognition.

When I talk about these voiceless needy people, I also refer to the fact that they lack a structured public representation in society. This lack of voice goes beyond family members and requires formal and structured representation at the social level. This is one of the most odious circumstances on which I have never heard a thorough debate by most of those who should actually be responsible, not just by virtue of holding the position but having the ability to exercise effective control over these issues.

It is time to act and ensure that the elderly receive the attention, respect, and assistance they deserve in a society that should be based on solidarity and the protection of the most vulnerable in the name of democracy and humanity. These have been some of my experiences dealing with various actors (families, guardians, cooperative administration, local public and private offices, etc.) in this social assistance sector, carried out under the pretext of solidarity.

Fraudulent Practices in the Cooperative Sector: A Thorough Analysis

This episode is yet another clear example of the distorted ethics that characterize most of the cooperatives I have come into contact with. This distorted ethics diverges completely from the true meaning of social solidarity. Through this distorted practice, cooperatives can easily hire unqualified personnel for delicate assignments in any area of their projects, without any consideration for the quality of services provided. However, when regulations from public administration force them to hire individuals with certified qualifications, their priority is often to select obedient individuals with low ambition and demands. Only later do they consider the issue of competence, which, unfortunately, always comes last. These unfair strategies prove harmful to most associated workers.

The oligarchies within the cooperatives prefer to interact with individuals aligned with their cynical ideology, as they believe this can limit debate. However, they overlook the fact that this same dynamic hinders productivity, innovation, and problem-solving. In other words, this mindset shows a lack of progressive orientation towards the future, neglecting rational management of the present. Qualified workers are sometimes recruited only to exploit their certifications to secure contracts. Although these candidates present qualification documents, they are later on deployed within the organization for different and less remunerative tasks. In the end, these associated collaborators undergo humiliations in various forms, designed to push them out of the cooperative after securing the contract they were seeking.

This situation can result in a voluntary decision of the employee to leave the organization or in a labour union-mediated dismissal, aiming to avoid controversy. This scenario is particularly common in projects related to immigration (reception projects), where the dismissal of a qualified mediator is often witnessed to be replaced by a refugee who has just learned little or nothing about where they are. Unfortunately, this dynamic is very common in various cooperatives.

It is a serious and widespread problem that language and cultural mediators face in many work situations. Mediation work is crucial to ensure effective communication between individuals who speak different languages or come from different cultures. However, often these figures do not receive the right economic and social consideration for the essential role they play. This situation of being considered outsiders by the oligarchs in the inclusion program does not help either the mediators or society in terms of problem-solving.

Language and cultural mediators face various challenges, including:

1) Inadequate compensation: Many times, the compensation offered does not reflect the importance of the work done and does not take into account the complexity of the issues they face;

2) Day or hourly work: Employment as daily or hourly workers can lead to significant economic insecurity and may reduce the interest in being seriously innovative in their work since they often do not enjoy long-term job security or benefits;

3) Emergency situations and pressure: Mediators are often called upon to handle complex and urgent situations, but their work may be undervalued and not adequately compensated;

4) Lack of recognition: They do not always receive the recognition they deserve for the crucial role they play in helping people overcome language and cultural barriers, etc.

A case of relevance and prominence is the so-called "black work" and professional impoverishment: recently, an immigrant family consisting of a husband, a wife, and a minor was hired by the cooperative. After the expiration of their contracts, the cooperative continued to illegally employ this family for years, exploiting them and relegating them to unpaid work. The family reported this situation to the police but has yet to receive a response from the competent authority, despite more than a year having passed. Cooperatives often portray themselves as benevolent entities, hiring foreigners or disadvantaged individuals under the pretext of social solidarity (which falls within the same context) with the intention of exploiting them with meagre salaries and stealing their working hours. Unfortunately, this scenario even leaves many qualified Italian professionals without job opportunities.

"Penny Wise and Pound Foolish" in the Cooperative: Damaging Choices for Social Solidarity

Within our cooperative, an emblematic episode occurred that illustrates the application of the English proverb "Penny wise and pound foolish," which, in their explanation, will be under the pretext that "practice makes perfect." In this case, a refugee, who has just had his refugee status granted without adequate professional qualification, was hired to replace three highly qualified maintenance workers. This decision was motivated by a short-term vision, where immediate economic savings took precedence over considering the long-term consequences. This example is emblematic of the short-sighted approach preventing the achievement of genuine social solidarity.

Those responsible for these choices seem to give little importance to the effectiveness of job execution. For them, acting as oligarchs, the main goal is to maintain control and pursue their selfish interests. This often translates into hiring low-cost labour based on the belief that those accepting reduced wages are more likely to obey, at the expense of skills and the effectiveness of services to be rendered.

This attitude causes damage to both the evolution of a progressive workforce in the community and the image of foreigners who accept these jobs. At the same time, it deprives competent Italians of culturally suitable job opportunities.

It is crucial to recognize that when an individual is paid less than they deserve for a promising long-term job, this creates a negative perspective. It denies the possibility of professional growth, the acquisition of necessary skills for progress, and the ability to contribute to the future workforce's competence. This situation not only represents wage injustice but also hinders the quality of human resources available for innovation, compromising the dignity of those involved.

To reverse this trend, it is essential to ensure fair compensation for the work done and provide the necessary support for training and professional growth. Only in this way can the potential of each worker be maximized, contributing to the organization's progress.

A concrete example I have encountered is the hiring of foreigners solely for economic reasons, to pay lower wages without facing relative inconveniences. However, this often leads to the employment of inadequately trained personnel in culturally sensitive roles, such as those in the field of social assistance. This practice can compromise rational efforts to promote the collective well-being of society and fruitful innovation for the society in question.

Often, these unqualified individuals lacking the appropriate cultural and professional training of their host country or without receiving further training or experiences absorbed into the system created by the oligarchs could not only limit growth prospects but also harm the society as a whole. For example, immigrants are always available and satisfied to accept lower wages. They do not complain. Evidently, they are humble due to their precarious situation, which doesn't really mean that they are willingly adhering to the system or being grateful to the host society for their sustenance received.

It is equally worrisome that these individuals do not have time to be adequately trained due to the hectic conditions of the workplace. Unfortunately, they will not even have time to be followed up, if not through mediocre supervision by some older workers in their workplace while carrying out their daily frenetic activities. At the same time, Italian professionals will be left out to make room for low-cost labour, creating an imbalanced situation (i.e., those with a specific cultural and professional background in Italy: this does not imply that they are better trained, but that the procedural system is different, creating a discrepancy in the job field).

This situation has serious consequences for the citizens of the middle/lower class in this society. It affects their rights to job security and opportunities, hinders their ability to express themselves, and limits their professional advancement from a low-level position to high or to an excellent position of competence and power.

It is even worse because it fuels a subtle but damaging conflict between oppressed classes (both immigrants and the middle/lower class and below). This is one of the major phenomena that have led to a form of racism perpetuated by this cooperative system. But it is difficult to understand for the governing class due to the growing gap of disparities between different social classes in today's contemporary society. By training, I mean social inclusion that includes comprehensive cultural and civic training. This happens while well-prepared Italians and old immigrants begin to lose their built-in work and citizenship capacity over the years. Or the only choice that might remain available to them is to become immigrants themselves in another country. This means social precariousness and impoverishment of society for all, citizens and foreigners alike.

As a result, end-users receive inadequate services, as workers (both foreigners and less privileged) are not adequately trained and cannot add value to society. The cooperative deprives these Italians and motivated old immigrants who have lived in the country for years of their dignity, opportunities, and responsibilities in terms of financial growth and innovation. In the first place, the cooperatives risk further promoting racism within the middle/lower classes, and secondly, they risk undermining the efficiency of the services offered, as workers are not adequately trained to add value to society. It is essential to provide cultural and civic training to facilitate social inclusion and to promote a fair growth environment.

This harmful attitude is reflected in the racial dispute that pervades this country in more artful and systematic ways. It is also one of the main causes hindering a society from achieving essential competitiveness for growth, in terms of product and innovative value without being subdued by others. It is important to consider the implications of these choices, as they can have lasting consequences on social cohesion and national competitiveness. Only through investments in training, fair compensation, and the promotion of a competent workforce will it be possible to build a more inclusive and productive society.

Therefore, in my opinion, society will suffer setbacks in development due to poor services provided by an inexperienced workforce. In this way, presumably, some other problems will be created, including:

1) foreigners will not be able to express themselves to the fullest extent;

2) Italians will not have their jobs for which they were culturally equipped to perform;

3) and ultimately, society will lack the potential to compete on the global stage in terms of productivity. This situation will become a cultural catastrophe in due course.

This attitude is also connected to the racial dispute present in the country today, but it is not just the type of racism as most of us would think. Cooperatives hire experts only if bureaucratically forced to do so, and even in those cases, in most situations, they would hire experts only to avoid bureaucratic difficulties. However, shortly after, these experts will be fired or humiliated by assigning them tasks that have nothing to do with their professional preparation. The problem is that oligarchs seek more money for themselves rather than for the good of society and do not care about the well-being of the same society itself. This is what pollutes the current bureaucratic system.

The Irony of Fate for Members and Needy in the Cooperative Context
The Cooperative in the Eyes of the Oligarchs

Today's cooperative has become a lucrative business for oligarchs, whose main purpose is the immoderate accumulation of wealth. Most of these entities seem to pay little attention to the reintegration of the sick, elderly, refugees, and generally those in need. These people are often considered only as part of a structure to be tolerated, as long as the situation does not become so severe as to threaten the cooperative's image. In such a case, measures will be taken to resolve the issue to their advantage. This reality seems to have been accepted; then, by chance, as part of cultural normality, just like a custom or habit of a people rooted in our society. This is usually how our daily reality is structurally formed. For most cooperatives, the needs of citizens and social challenges have become synonymous with financial gain. The few cooperatives that maintain social awareness are often suffocated, both by the corrupt majority and the bureaucracy that, ironically, was originally conceived to combat corruption. This dynamic, developed over time, has proven to be an obstacle for those with good intentions and trying to operate ethically. It almost seems like a situation of "if you can't beat them, join them." NOTE: In the long run, as is already happening, some cooperatives operating honestly might find themselves forced to close. This is because they may not be able to sustain this unfavourable policy, while others may succumb to the system itself. These realities risk not surviving as they become victims of the cumbersome bureaucracy, which has in the meantime become the only means of defence available to public administration to address its own weaknesses. A lesson I have drawn from my experiences is that often "people are so focused on the future that they end up neglecting the present." A truly deplorable situation. Finally, the situation of psychiatric patients is nothing more than a business for many cooperatives; as long as the patients stay with them, the more stable and prolonged the income for the cooperatives themselves. When cooperatives boast about job placement for disabled people, it might seem like an altruistic gesture, but it could actually hide exploitation. Often these people are forced to work for minimal wages or, in some cases, no pay at all, such as in componential employment. This situation raises many concerns.

Health Risk for Cooperative Members

I have observed numerous associated workers leave, despite having high productivity capabilities that the cooperative could have exploited. Some left before the situation deteriorated too much, proving lucky. Those who stayed beyond what was due faced the nightmare of insecurity and, in some cases, were engulfed by a self-imposed borderline personality necessary for their survival. *This situation is akin to those who today seek refuge in psychotropic drugs due to a psychological pathology of obscure origin, as some former colleagues have told me. I, too, found myself at risk of developing a borderline personality, and I fought desperately to bring about a change in my current situation. This book has become an outlet for me. Today, I can attest to numerous cases of former colleagues who are under medical therapy. I refer to those who tried to face the chaos they were in on their own, to those who sought solutions to their real problem. I am not talking about those who could not understand and those who could not afford the time and financial consequences necessary to solve their problem. In the end, some of these people were strong enough to withstand the test of time; they become like them for the 'effect of cultural annihilation.'* The cooperative formula, which was proposed to help society solve its social dilemmas, has instead turned into a source of additional problems. While those responsible for this situation try to hide the mess they have created; buying political and financial paths and coexisting with an unsustainable system that they should have helped change. In short, these cooperative oligarchs coexist with an unsustainable system that they should have helped reform.

The Hermetically Sealed Cooperative

I have never seen an organization as hermetically protected as the one I worked for, devoid of internal transparency. A triumvirate of executives holds decision-making power over every aspect, even the most insignificant matters. This tight grip on management prevents anyone from making correct decisions within the work environment, including associated workers (i.e., members) and coordinators of different sessions. Consequently, every situation is resolved through their final decision, slowing down action, fuelling confusion, and discouraging the perfection of professional skills. Services that should be provided to our clients are delayed or even interrupted. The three executives, overwhelmed by their sometimes-overloaded tasks, struggle to manage the situations. Their actions are guided by greed, to the detriment of the effectiveness and efficiency of our services, thereby damaging both society and those in greater need. There are among us individuals who need support to face their precarious situations, yet the executives continue to prioritize their thirst for profit over what would be just and necessary.

The Insignificance of Skills

Throughout the period I operated as a collaborator (member) in this cooperative, I never had the opportunity to observe any form of strategic planning for collective and continuous interest for long-term goals. Everything seemed to be orchestrated internally at the main headquarters, including the shifts of workers in various sectors. This happened without consulting the respective coordinators of different projects, except for some sectors led by those who unconditionally answered only 'yes sir' to the president. Oligarchies were the only ones with the authority to negotiate on every issue, even if they often showed an inadequate understanding of the details on which they had to make decisions. A competent collaborator was never assigned to supervise operations in their field of expertise. This often led to the insertion of unreliable individuals like them, who could easily exploit their positions to gain personal benefits, even at the expense of the oligarchs themselves. Such associated workers were involved in activities that emptied the cooperative of everything they could lay their hands on, siphoning off any accessible resources, as a way to survive. It is as if "the upright heart pays the hardest price for heartless people," as the saying goes. Today, this society seems to have fallen under a spell, trapping the poor citizens in a cycle of silent suffering concealed by fake smiles. I think only a few courageous souls could challenge this antisocial system, while many of us are already destined to succumb, without any other choice. Meanwhile, those of us who resist must be ready to pay the price to preserve our dignity, in the name of humanity. In my experience, I have never encountered a work environment where coordinators or professionals were present only to meet bureaucratic needs. Coordinators had no say in the structuring of their own departments. Often, the heads had informants within various projects (these so-called collaborators had more say than the coordinators), individuals who, in reality, had more decision-making power than the coordinators themselves. This dynamic is useful only to maintain the power of the leaders, but it has not been beneficial for the progress of the projects or for the well-being of the associated workers or the services that were supposed to be provided. Consider some emblematic cases: a general safety security officer that was transferred from her role of competence to janitor; a maintenance coordinator that was moved to the position of a driver; an office that is having three receptionists almost at work always simultaneously; a structure where service shifts were assigned by the central office without consulting the project coordinators; a vehicle maintenance worker in the cooperative who is struggling even to drive her own car, let alone service vehicles, due to organizational inefficiency. In this scenario, a problem of poorly managed business administration and internal communication emerges. People are moved without any criterion, thus losing any opportunity for professional growth, development, and enhancement of their skills. It is evident that the cooperative sometimes tries to please certain individuals, perhaps for their loyalty to the oligarchies, but this creates organizational chaos at the expense of overall efficiency. In conclusion, we face a crucial question: is cooperation based on collaboration and reciprocity, or does the will of internal powers prevail? It almost seems like we are simple subjects to the oligarchs as in medieval feudal courts, fighting among ourselves instead of collaborating. This situation is far from the true essence of work. Leftist parties, which have solidarity as their ideological foundation, have consistently worked to keep the cooperative alive and to support every financial request with the hope that the situation improves. In contrast, these oligarchs, who are forcefully present in the political arena, do not care about any political ideology or a political program except for their selfish interests. This demonstrates a lack of social responsibility and a denial of the values of solidarity that should underlie every political decision related to social issues. Certainly, their interests are cantered only on making money more easily without too much concern, unlike what would be found in the private sector. Furthermore, the leadership of some cooperatives, instead of promoting the well-being of associated workers (members), mostly focuses their attention on those they have marked as opponents or critics of their projects. This attitude, although it may seem an attempt to ensure efficiency and protect the interests of the cooperative, actually creates tensions and difficulties among the workers themselves. However, the real problem is that this attitude favours the interest of a few at the expense of the collective individuals. The oligarchies have never shown interest in the well-being of workers, working conditions, or the interests of the cooperative and society. Instead, they act only to preserve their illicit personal gains, ignoring the common good. These oligarchs use any excuse at their disposal to divert attention from their illicit affairs.

Composition of the Board of Directors (BOD)

Take, for example, the composition of the BOD: The BOD is composed of personalities selected for their loyalty to the President, without considering the necessary requirements in terms of competence and ethics in social solidarity or seniority, if any. The BOD has become a perfect bureaucratic formula for the personal enrichment of the oligarchs. Psychologically, these individuals selected by the president's inner circle consider themselves fortunate to be among the chosen ones for the positions they find themselves holding, not for their personal merit, such as in the BOD, and they even boast about it! It seems that the cooperative has become fertile ground for emphasizing personal interests at the expense of the primary goal of promoting solidarity and collective growth.

The Convocation of the Cooperative's Ruin for Members, But Not for the Oligarchs

Due to a considerable gap, both in terms of physical distance and communicative distance, between the central office and various sectors of the cooperative, combined with an antisocial atmosphere and the oligarchs' intention to concentrate all activities in their hands, a deep rift has formed. This division has caused a void, a lack of communication and coordination among the involved parties.

As things progressed, the situation deteriorated. Honest and hardworking collaborators were subtly expelled in a scenario orchestrated by the oligarchs themselves. The cooperative had to deal with unscrupulous and heartless individuals skilled at manipulating social dynamics to their advantage.

At that point, I began to foresee the imminent risk of uncontrolled expenses and ineffective human resource management within the organization. I then deduced in advance that now or later, this problem was going to strike hard on all the members of the cooperative.

I tried to sound the alarm by speaking to the oligarchs personally. However, as often happens, my words were not taken seriously enough.

Therefore, before the summer of 2021, rumours started circulating within the cooperative about the loss of most of our contracts with most of the public administrations and some other private sectors. This was a warning sign. Complaints were already accumulating from external partners regarding the inadequate services offered by our cooperative, as well as from employees who were complaining about the oligarchs' management regime.

Fear among the associated workers was palpable. The threat of a crisis loomed over the cooperative, which could jeopardize the employments of many.

When I personally tried to raise my concerns with the oligarchs, they were quick to deny everything, labelling the rumours as mere gossip. However, they acknowledged that there were operational challenges but downplayed the situation, assuring me that everything would be resolved. Shortly after our meeting, a general assembly was convened to discuss the difficulties the cooperative was facing.

The Downfall of the Cooperative

In any case, I know that "the end will surely justify the means"; so, let its Revelation come. In fact, I was not wrong; between the end of 2021 and the beginning of 2022, the cooperative suffered a massive collapse.

Urgently, something had to be done, and I am already doing my part by sharing my experiences. I decided to share my experience, attempting to raise awareness and at least offer my testimony, which is the most I could afford. The situation had become critical and required immediate intervention. A serious reform in the field of social solidarity would be necessary to reverse the destructive trend.

The experience of intellectual vigour teaches us that where discipline and merit-based recognition are lacking, ethics fades, and innovation dwindles. Without investment in skills and sustainable development, the inevitable outcome is ruin.

I will briefly try to summarize the content of this ASSEMBLY meeting, highlighting the most relevant elements. Irony emerges when the circumstantial voices, which had been denied and concealed by the oligarchs, turned into reality for the cooperative. Their plans had been set in motion for some time. On the assembly meeting day, they once again convinced us to give them part of our annual earnings so that they could accumulate ulterior funds to be used as a financial reserve for the future contract security to meet bureaucratic requirements. They did actually rob us of our money by their usual tricks, and shortly after, the cooperative's contracts began to crumble.

This was a low blow, a massive deception against all of us. Some of us were fired, others laboriously transferred to other cooperatives, while others were demoted or had their working hours cut. During the meeting, these above-written actions were never mentioned, not even once, that any of us would lose his or her job with the cooperative. But we were only asked to support the cooperative with a portion of our earnings so that they could collect some funds as a financial reserve for the tenders of the coming year, 2022 contracts. In fact, there was more emphasis on why we should all raise this fund, which would serve to secure our jobs and prevent any form of downsizing. Even though this situation was very uncomfortable for everyone, they decided to carry it out through existing wrong procedures supported by the power and provisional veto of the Board of Directors (BOD). So, "we are all worker-members in theory, but only a handful of them could decide the fate of all of us in the cooperative."

They had planned this strategy well in advance to rob us of our hard-earned money and our democratic rights. The promises made to maintain our jobs in exchange for money donations turned out to be false and empty. We personally witnessed the realization of what we feared. Those who had promised otherwise denied any responsibility and continued to take our money by force of the use of a bureaucratic falsehood.

In summary, we underwent compromises that were not honoured. We were deprived of our earnings without any compensation in return. It's hard to accept that when things go wrong, the weakest pay the price, but when there is profit, only a few enjoy abundance.

Within a few months of this meeting, their tricks were revealed: after putting together and collecting most of our money, the cooperative lost a large part of its contracts, something the oligarchs were already aware of several months before the spread of the rumours. It was a colossal fraud against us!

In any case, the oligarchies remain firmly in their place, enjoying the wealth accumulated by the cooperative. And, even more unpleasantly, they robbed us of our earnings before definitively ousting us.

I often wonder, "How does this system reconcile with social solidarity?" I tried to confront the oligarchs again, but without success. I chose to share my painful experience with society as a whole, trying to bring out the human aspect in the face of such challenges. I also tried to involve the labour union, various lawyers, and my former colleagues to take legal action against this fraudulent act but often encountered resistance due to their personal and institutional weaknesses in the face of the powerful positions held by the oligarchs.

CONCLUSIVE SUMMARY

I would like to emphasize clearly that my assertive criticism should not be misunderstood as a critique based on "morality" or "human behaviour" within an individualistic context compared to the rest of the world. Instead, I want to focus on human relationships within the parameters of 'social solidarity.' This concept is closely linked to ethics and the definition of what social solidarity should represent conceptually, so that it can come to life in the shared reality of a civil society regulated by laws and regulations.

I am not interested in strictly defined idle comforts or superficial orientation. I am not even seeking so-called "righteous vanity." This is my human struggle against our collectivistic societal ailment, redirecting our ambitions towards reconstruction, reconciliation, cooperation, and peace for all. Primarily, I am committed to an innovative system of 'social assistance' that can help the needy and ensure a sustainable future for the generations to come. This is my open advocacy for the needy and the poor citizens among us, who are often voiceless and underrepresented in public life.

Sometimes, from the depths of my heart, I wonder: 'what is the benefit for an individual to gain the whole world and lose his or her own soul,' as the Bible says? I refer to losing oneself in the insignificant void of this temporary life that we already know. Everything I have recounted so far is based on personal experiences and direct testimonies, but I have also heard of many other atrocities committed against the needy and voiceless. This represents only a small part of the entire deceptive structure of this system. A system that the majority avoids discussing or obstructing for fear of compromising their own security or personal selfishness in pursuing daily survival.

Despite this, each of us possesses some knowledge of these issues, even if only in part. So, there is nothing new or hidden from everyday reality within this cooperative working context. It is urgent to reform this system, or it will continue to enrich only the oligarchs at the expense of the entire population. There is an urgent need for a strategic and social structure suitable for the present times needs to be developed.

To clarify any misunderstandings: here in this country, most of the courses I attended, organized by cooperatives, were purely formal and served primarily to inflate fictitious expenses. The cooperative system, as it stands today, exploits the private and public sectors too much, which could otherwise provide quality services and competitiveness in innovative sectors.

In the end, the current situation has always ultimately been attributed to the government's inability to intervene with adequate rules and reforms that can create a structure different from this cumbersome and dependent bureaucracy, which is now the subject of general complaints.

We must remember the reasons that led to the decline of real socialism and carefully reflect on whether we should encourage such a system without considering its pros and cons. The partial decentralization of social services management from public authorities to local cooperatives does not solve social problems but temporarily hides them. This approach allows or enables politicians, especially at the local level, to evade direct responsibility for the situation.

However, it is evident that cooperatives receiving contracts from local authorities to perform activities that should be carried out by municipal social assistants employed by themselves will never be free to help the needy according to their issues without political decision behind the scenes, as this could jeopardize their contracting access to/with the local public offices. It would be preferable for assistance to be directly provided by the social workers employed by the public sector for job security and for unbiased decision to be assured. This would eliminate the fear of losing jobs by cooperative social workers and losing contracts by the cooperatives themselves.

Is it right for a mayor to work as an employee of the cooperative in his community and that also on a contract with the same municipality where he holds an administrative role? This is a strange world made up of various interconnections! In this situation, a serious conflict of interest arises. The services that should be offered by the cooperative in question are compromised both due to financial issues related to their provision and personal influence.

Moreover, I have noticed that many people who should receive assistance as true disabled individuals struggle to access the benefits they are entitled to for their livelihood. Concrete actions should be taken to address these issues and ensure that services are offered fairly and justly to all those in need.

In conclusion, I state that bureaucracy in a democratic government system is redundant for self-defence. This is because it seems that the system is designed to favour those who already have power and resources, creating greater obstacles for those with less. This makes the lower classes even more dependent on the privileged classes.

In summary: 'It is said that 'a story could only make sense if it is told in its entirety.' 'The power behind fantasy lies in recognizing deeply the reality.'

Contradictions due to redundant bureaucracy and the cooperative system

Evidence indicates that some people receive government assistance even if they may not actually need it or deserved it. Among them are individuals who pretend to be disabled, cleverly exploiting every opportunity to get help. At the same time, there are those who have family support or a better understanding of bureaucratic procedures, which are often intricate.

On the other hand, there are needy individuals who receive assistance from cooperatives and unions. These organizations offer legal and bureaucratic support to defend these individuals' rights but at a considerable cost. This can be advantageous for the needy but can also represent a financial burden for the state, which is simultaneously attributed as funding in favour of the needy but mainly ends up in the coffers of the same organizations. Unlike cooperatives, unions (like labour unions) are a separate case due to their knowledge, expertise, and collective influence rooted over time, which adds to their advantage.

This can be seen as an advantage for the needy, but at the same time can represent a financial burden for the state, which is attributed as funding in favour of the needy but mainly ends up in the coffers of the same organizations. In any case, the issue of money seems to dominate always, both for those receiving assistance and for the cooperatives providing it. It would be crucial to carefully assess the needs of the needy and ensure that support is distributed fairly and justly, without the presence of an oppressive bureaucratic system which has to mainly be of more advantage to the middle personalities or organizations.

In conclusion, there is a risk that most truly needy people are constantly excluded. Often, those who are seriously ill do not admit their condition and never ask for help. Similarly, those living in poverty or abandonment may not have the resources or knowledge necessary to seek assistance from public authorities, which often do not provide aid unless explicitly requested for and more over it has to be applied for through a third party designate by the state itself. These individuals are often overlooked due to their disadvantaged situation.

I will not stop reiterating that cooperatives seem more interested in maintaining appearances (referring to corrupt oligarchies) and avoiding problems with public authorities, accumulating only "bureaucratic credits" to easily participate in tenders. The rest seems to have no value for them, as this system works perfectly to their advantage. As long as these bureaucratic aspects are regulated for a change from the way they are now, the situation will remain unchanged.

I have always wondered what the connection is between this redundant clumsiness of regulations and bureaucratic organization with the provision of essential services to the needy. It has long been known that, for the proper functioning of cooperatives, they should draw lessons from experiences and initiatives already implemented in the field, using functional problem-solving plans and strategies as a basis for progressive innovation. However, those who have direct experience of these situations are the associated workers, theoretically called "members," with their collective will. Unfortunately, such workers are often undervalued and relegated to the background, deprived of decision-making power within the cooperative. As a result, many valuable experiences are lost.

These workers are often the first to be laid off due to conflicts of interest between the desire for social development and the greed for money and power of the oligarchies. I constantly wonder if there has ever been a stable strategic objective through the implementation of innovative plans. On the contrary, I have noticed that the cooperative has mainly focused on vainglorious narratives regarding relationships established with mayors, local authorities, politicians, and high-ranking public administration staff, as well as with other associated cooperatives.

Furthermore, I have noticed how the cooperatives have often exploited varied influences to manipulate the system of various influential sectors available to obtain contracts and maintain tenders. I am not opposed to these relationships at all, but I am concerned about their impact on social services provided to the needy and on social solidarity, which should be the end product of cooperative activities. It would be vital for the cooperative to focus more on defining clear strategic objectives and implementing innovative plans to improve the social services offered.

I wonder always if this corrupt attitude is really necessary to make the business related to "social solidarity" work and if we are really doing our duty in the right way for humanity, which is at the core of the concept of social solidarity itself. An oligarch once declared that competence does not matter and that it is better to learn doing the job. This approach seems contradictory, as a worker should possess at least basic skills to perform their job before they can improve on them. I later understood that their main goal is not the creation of sustainable work from a human and financial point of view, focused on solidarity.

Interestingly, they never offer the opportunity for those with solidarity intentions to be part of their illicit inclination. To survive in this scenario, cooperation with cooperatives is essential, but only if it voluntarily contributes to the system without receiving remuneration. For example, adopting the principle of giving and receiving in terms of solidarity seems to be considered an undesirable prerequisite for becoming a member of the cooperative elite. I can testify to many cases of people I collaborated with within the cooperative. When they joined, they were enthusiastic, but they left sick, weak, and disappointed, as if they had lived in a realm of deceit or devil. The more these oligarchies concentrate powers in their hands for their own interests, the more they move away from the foundation of cooperative reality and the issue of social solidarity! In conclusion, I want to state that anyone who thinks what I have written is false and if someone intends to sue me, he or she should do so as an individual, but not using the resources from associations or cooperatives. It is important to understand what it means to fight for one's rights with one's personal resources and knowledge. In case of misunderstandings or inaccuracies, I invite anyone to contact me for a civil debate. I am open to any form of communication that can facilitate a constructive and collaborative dialogue, as this my deposition is in everyone's interest to ensure the accuracy of the factual information presented in this book.

My reaction based on my positive experiences

NOTE: From 2015 to the beginning of 2020, I dedicated intense effort to researching more effective methods for managing the phenomenon of refugees and hospitality. I transitioned from a generic approach to a strategy adapted to the context of the country where I reside. Over time, I made significant progress in this area. However, my next goal is to further delve into these issues.

It should be emphasized that I also invested time in assisting needy individuals. I often observed counterproductive attitudes regarding therapy and social reintegration of people into the social environment. This observation led me to reflect on the importance of considering the diverse social and cultural realities of individuals and adapting therapies and reintegration strategies to their specific needs and contexts.

From my experiences, it emerges that our assumptions often do not align with the concrete results of actions, even in the most promising cases. Consequently, collaboration is necessary to face the challenges of existence and adapt to the reality presented, even if it may seem unsustainable.

What makes everything interesting is that no one truly has absolute control over reality because reality needs to be seen with an approach of both cultural and personal diversity. Our mood influences our way of acting in the world of existence, and that is what truly matters, beyond the results obtained. Each of us is the product of the lived experiences of our existence, and every individual should feel responsible for contributing to the construction and promotion of a social system that expresses the power of creation.

ETHICS OF COOPERATIVE MISINTERPRED

I want to be unequivocal on one point: I do not intend to teach how to establish a cooperative or demonstrate my moral correctness. Instead, I want to highlight the inconsistencies I have encountered in the actual functioning of this system. The disconcerting situation is not simply about naivety or ignorance; it is rather the perpetuation of a diabolical system that acts against the collectivity of real people.

If cooperation is indeed a conducive condition for any meaningful, logical, and effective freedom, then it must flourish through a form of mutual aid that modulates the interaction between living beings over time and space, in harmony with the cultural evolution, the political and social orientation of a society.

As a result, cooperatives need real control by public institutions, which should exercise this role not in a purely bureaucratic or formal manner, but with authentic oversight. This would prevent the needy and the poor from becoming easy victims of the ambitions of cooperative oligarchs, who act in the name of 'social solidarity' intentions but often pursue their own personal interests.

Therefore, in this country, as in many parts of the world from ancient times, there is a structural awareness of new forms of cooperation primarily oriented towards the needy, guided by a spirit of deep community solidarity in different places.

The cooperative enterprise should arise from the aspiration for solidarity through social entrepreneurship, respecting human dignity and not fuelling private selfishness that has concretized. This entrepreneurial motivation should draw from the desire to contribute to the intelligence, industriousness, and initiative for the benefit of the community.

However, after all said regarding to the generally known prospective of the cooperative as dream, the reality has led the facts to a distorted situation where, when things go wrong, the usual individuals (the needy, the members, and the society) bear the consequences, while the oligarchs remain excluded and seem to live in a separate dimension. Meanwhile, it is precisely the same oligarchs who unilaterally determine the social destiny of the cooperative system, often to satisfy their selfish interests. This behaviour contributes to exacerbating problems rather than solving them, as it is a strategic way to enrich only their classes.

I have noticed that the most popular phrase is "cooperation in love is the game," but reality often shows that the contrary is the normality on ground. Those who practice what they preach often find themselves being sacrifices, almost like sacrificial figures: such as the character of Jesus in its symbolic guise.

For about 7 years (2015-2022), I collaborated consistently with this cooperative. However, no meeting was ever held to discuss concretely how to invest independently in human resources, except for theoretical propaganda purposes or to improve financial coverage at a bureaucratic level. Only meetings were organized to participate in programs between cooperatives, aimed at conforming to the existing system or enlarging the portfolio of oligarchs by participating in their assignments within an ideological context of play.

If anyone is willing to work without compensation, contribute financially, or dedicate their time, or if someone presents any proposal aimed at securing financial advantages, that individual will always be warmly embraced by the oligarchies that profit from every conceivable angle. However, if the cooperative needs to invest in exploring innovations, this surely becomes a forbidden zone. There is a cliché to respect, based on the dictatorship of the oligarch.

In my opinion, the current view of cooperatives represents a distortion from the values of social solidarity. There is a lack of a human-cantered purpose, transforming the cooperative into a mechanism that boost private investments influenced by political and external dynamics, camouflaged under the name of 'cooperative.'

Cooperatives talk a lot but act too little and easily succumb to inertia and proactive ambition. I believe that volunteering and philanthropy should be distinct from the cooperative system. This commingling has become a hidden platform for oligarchs, who play an illicit game on it. This approach does not promote achieving the goals of social justice; it is challenging to make correct decisions when there are two operating modes of participations (paid personalities and voluntary personalities) in the provision of sensitive services for which cooperatives receive compensations.

It is evident that voluntary work has great social value and plays a viable role in favour of the most vulnerable with a non-profit approach. However, the cooperative should be a democratically managed enterprise of social solidarity, based on a solid ethical status. Unfortunately, I have seen few cooperatives structured in this way, judging from how things are managed behind closed doors, according to my experience.

The goal of the cooperative is supposed to be collective well-being, even in the context of small groups, through the ethics of social solidarity. This does not exclude that collective action could generate individual benefits of an economic nature, such as a stable income derived from cooperative work. In other words, the cooperative believes should be that collaboration and sharing of resources can improve both collective and individual well-being without sacrificing one for the other.

After all these reflections, it remains important to remain faithful to the ethics underlying these intentions on behalf of true solidarity. However, unfortunately, this is not today's reality. Most cooperative solidarity associations have turned into sick and speculative entities, as clearly evident from the currently narrated situation that I have to live with for years.

A reform and adequate control are urgent to continue dreaming of the resolutions and intentions that initially inspired cooperatives. These actions could breathe vitality into cooperation between individuals, in the true sense of social solidarity, with tangible results in operational terms with concrete facts.

Within the cooperative, I have noticed that the oligarchies pay more attention to the bureaucratic compliance required by public authorities and show reverence towards such authorities, not respect for the actual laws themselves. However, social problems that should be at the centre of attention are often neglected. This happens because the real operators in the field are not necessarily the social figures that appear daily in the mainstream media at the forefront to discuss possible structural solutions to social challenges.

In my view, in the absence of innovation, there will also be a lack of progressive proposals from cooperatives to public institutions to improve efficiency, effectiveness, and sustainability. However, financial demands always persist, as does the increase in bureaucracy that is choking the system. In the end, the barrier that the governmental system wanted to break down is becoming more complicated to overcome.

At this point, the hope of relying on cooperatives to fill social gaps in the society's welfare system seems almost like a fantastic dream deprived of social improvement.

The True Consolidated Strategy

The individuals in power within cooperatives, the oligarchs, are exploiting their privileges to gain profits. This occurs through the use of bureaucratic manoeuvres combined with fictitious budgets, all with the goal of consolidating their position and making the community increasingly dependent on them, meanwhile accumulating wealth and influence.

The relationship between cooperatives and public entities in this country has been based on dynamics of 'false ideological belonging' and deceptive compromises, loosely tied to legality. This has disseminated clientelism instead of preventing it through periodic checks, as originally intended when the cooperatives were established.

The president of a cooperative is always powerful and wealthy (but masks this condition with a false appearance of poverty). However, they often hide their true condition behind a fictitious appearance. They are not recognized for their innovative capacity or for promoting revolutionary initiatives for the benefit of the community, but rather for their questionable complicity with some politicians who share similar objectives. This complicity exists independently of political views or affiliation.

A well-known fact is that if someone tries to take legal action against these oligarchies, they will be countered with all the means available from the cooperative's funds, while the accuser will fight for their rights with their own resources. For this reason, everyone is avoiding a direct confrontation with them.

The oligarchs compensate for all damages they cause with the funds of the cooperative, which should belong to all the associate members. This cooperative system could be compared to a separate entity or an entity within another entity, similar to a state within a state.

Loss of Direction by the State in This Complicated Situation

Probably and initially, assigning some social problems to cooperatives may have provided relief to public administration in terms of human resources and efforts. However, over time, attention to these problems became diminished compared to the initial motivations of the cooperative pioneers, from the post-war period to the 1980s.

Currently, it seems that the state has lost the overall vision of the cooperative phenomenon relating to social issues and has lost the ability to manage the development and restructuring of the social problems afflicting the society. This is because the situation has been delegated to cooperatives for too long.

Today, we cling to a vague sense of solidarity derived from the 1970s and 1980s, based mainly on goodwill. However, the current cooperative model dates back to the 1970s and 1980s, while the economic and social situation has changed dramatically. In that period, there was a strong push for action, giving, helping, and cooperating for the common good of the entire population. But those times have passed, and idealizing them today is futile.

This has made it difficult at this moment in time to implement reforms, especially due to the involvement of cooperative presidents in politics, after accumulating wealth and influence. Undoubtedly, even if it is legitimate behaviour, it can be problematic for society as a whole, considering the potential conflict between their interests and those of the community itself.

I believe that relying solely on past experiences is ineffective and limiting. It is necessary to keep an open mind for learning and allow space for experimenting with new approaches that adapt to an evolving reality. We must maintain the humble hunger for learning and ensure that theoretically brilliant initiatives produce tangible and factual results that could serve our coexistence in an increasingly complex, dynamic, and progressive society. This is particularly important when dealing with the challenges of a population in a constantly changing social environment. These challenges must be addressed from infinite perspectives, with specific goals to manage our existential destiny in the best possible way.

Furthermore, public administration is disoriented with time in solving the complex situation of social assistance, which evolves rapidly over time. This is partly due to the politicians' detachment from the common population way of life, being focused on their own class as how to sustain it. Finally, the lobby of the cooperative union and associations represents an additional obstacle to changing the current system.

The initial proposals for the establishment of cooperatives were valid to reach those in need of genuine social support. It would then be appropriate to directly listen to those people who are the recipients of this support, namely the operators, not only the so-called "office of the president or the cooperative associates." Over time, these individuals have become subservient to the will of the cooperatives' oligarchies, accepting those that have already compromised their human self-esteem and values for their daily bread which doesn't really mean all that it takes to live a real life to survive while they are cunningly trapped in the inhuman system.

Most of them have become patients in need of care and support for a syndrome to which I would like to give a name like "identity misrepresentation." Thus, a deeper social decay is created in the society.

Therefore, meeting the needs of the population and the community through the responsibility of human sensitivity, combined with skills, should represent an entity aiming for a high degree of democracy, a model of "participatory democracy" and transparency. However, often these words remain only in theory and in rhetorical propaganda.

Cooperatives should be accountable to members and public administration in an innovative and continuous way, demonstrating with concrete facts their responsibility in providing social services for the benefit of the entire community. Transparency should be ensured through constant availability of accounting, social books, and budgets at the end of each year for accurate and careful consultation. Unfortunately, more often these pieces of information are read hastily and distractedly, perhaps during social recreative moments. Also, every year, we are asked to give up dividends as a sign of further contributions to the prosperity of the cooperative to ensure our job security and its continuity.

It is crucial to emphasize that many decisions made by oligarchies have always ignored the interests of the associate members and the community itself. These decisions are often motivated by veiled threats to make members feel indebted to the oligarchies themselves.

In reality, all members should have the right to access information about the cooperative's accounting and budgets, so they can consciously participate in decisions and strategic choices. Only in this way can an environment of transparency and fairness be created within the cooperative, where each member has the opportunity to contribute to the organization's success and earn their own daily livelihood without feeling like they have been saved by these fake "heroes of survival."

I have noticed that most explanatory articles written to describe our services and activities during the year were always manipulated to make them difficult to understand, especially by collaborators.

The values of a cooperative should be based on the purpose of achieving the well-being of the people and improving life in a given society. This should be through collective effort for the completion of initiatives in synergy with innovation, according to the dynamic evolution of civil society, involving everyone. Most cooperatives I know do not respect that fundamental link between members, which defines their collaborative strength, and the commendable interventions of associated initiatives. In particular, there is no practical operation based on respect for the individual capacities of members.

In all these years of my experience in the cooperative, I still lack the ability to see a real conjugation or collaboration between solidarity and economic value. The character of a social intervention for the good of the community should be closely linked to ideals, ethical approaches, rich in innovative research and continuity, with the need for a dynamically existential cultural mobility to achieve a real and tangible operation.

Purpose and Integrity of Cooperatives

What is the primary purpose of a cooperative in this country other than engaging in winning a contract for economic purposes? Is it justifiable only for these reasons?

1) Earning from a service already provided by public administration;

2) Earning from a service never before performed by the cooperative itself;

3) Earning from a service that the cooperative does not intend to continue offering

continuously after obtaining the contract and exploiting only the economic interest.
In my opinion, this behaviour seems to go against the ethical and moral logic of the utopian ideals underlying the creation of a solidarity cooperative.

Cooperative as a Special Enterprise

The social solidarity cooperative is a different type of enterprise compared to those of the private sector, as it should ensure greater security for workers and real assistance to society. However, it is equally possible for a cooperative to turn into a refuge for legalized illicit practices, such as looting the material assets of the community and perpetrating abuses of human rights of voiceless individuals, facilitated by various types of favouritism, thus requiring an effective control structure.
This statement indicates that the cooperative is governed by a complex bureaucratic system but has the advantage of obtaining contracts and easily participating in bids without individual, collective, or financial risks. Every risk should fall under the legal competence of the oligarchies for the personal actions taken on behalf of the cooperative's associated workers. However, this is often not the case. In reality, associated workers (called members) are disadvantaged. They are the ones who will suffer the consequences of any wrong decision made by the cooperative first: in a situation

when the cooperation fails to provide job opportunities. They cannot intervene in any situation, despite their expertise, unlike the Board of Directors (BOD) with its members chosen by the President in his favour.

I fear that this legitimate and dignified label of "COOPERATIVE" is starting to evolve over time and space as a true tumour of today's society. In other words, it risks becoming a precursor to future social decay. This term "cooperative," with its collective connotation, should be re-evaluated to return to the full conception of empathy and unity, to support the weaker citizens and the nature that surrounds us. Only in this way can we overcome the current situation of degradation!

MY CRITICAL OBSERVATIONS, IDEAS, AND SOLUTIONS IN BRIEF

My critical observations 'unconsciously false representation'

I would like to share some of my criticisms and observations on this topic, reflecting on what I have learned working as a cultural/linguistic mediator in the social world. When a dispute cannot be resolved, and both parties seem to lack reason simultaneously, it is often necessary to determine which of them is more powerful in terms of the authority in charge of running the collective governing system. This later should be the body to be more considerate in re-evaluating its position in the conflict. In my upcoming book on compensation and sustainable inclusion in terms of immigration, I will further develop this concept.

Undoubtedly, the lack of professional ethics that I have encountered in most of these centres has been disconcerting. This is clearly reflected in the precarious situation of associated operators, who often do not enjoy a stable permanent employment contract. The so-called "members" are made powerless in the face of humiliating treatments, starting from low wages and continuing with the authoritarian imposition of numerous obligations, devoid of any margin of choice. Most of them remain silent because they have no alternatives and are forced to accept compromises to survive. These individuals often end up becoming the true victims, who now require treatment for a pathology that could be defined as "unconsciously false representation," thus contributing to the deterioration of social structure.

Furthermore, there is a lack of clear indications regarding how operators should carry out their duties, and the figure of a competent representative from the sector is often absent. On the contrary, the representative among the workers is often chosen from those preferred or liked by the president, which is never based on competence. To further complicate the situation, I have noticed that within some cooperatives' workforces, workers receive a salary of just €300 at the end of a long month of work, despite the numerous responsibilities they carry. This scenario seems to operate almost under a control similar to that of criminal gangs: so that no one can say anything out of fear of retaliation.

After examining all these issues, I wondered how an operator in this field of social solidarity could be productive in such a situation. Especially considering that their work directly concerns our social well-being and the progression of our culture, starting from a solid long-term training foundation.

In a cooperative, those in power often act in isolation, preserving the opacity of political dynamics, similar to what happens within a criminal gang.

The 'Mafia' as Connotation and the Presidential Power of the Cooperative

The term "mafioso" is universally associated with criminal associative patterns, extending from the Italian reality to a phenomenon that has impacted many countries worldwide. Among these, there was a resonated news in Italy a few years ago about the 'capital mafia,' which involved a fraudulent act of a cooperative in Rome. However, it should be noted that there are also forms of mafia rooted in the North of the country, less discussed but equally impactful. These vary based on the cultural environments in which they operate but share the same goal of attaining power and accumulating wealth through dubious means.

This is my idea of what the Italian mafia is in different terms, from my cultural perspective: The Southern mafia, influenced by its history and culture, differs from the northern version. The former is characterized by a deep sense of omertà and respect for the sacredness of blood as a symbol of brotherhood in a religious way, while the latter is based on superficiality and economic greed. Both forms share opposition to common interests, involving illicit and harmful activities for society and its victims. Despite the differences, even the Northern mafia, although not based on blood ties, is equally condemnable for its actions that undermine social fabric. Ultimately, it causes the same and slow death to its victims ("dead man walking" and 'death postponed in the long term').

The oligarchies responsible for cooperatives often guard their experiences exclusively within the family circle and among those who share their interests. Heirs and perpetual representatives are appointed to maintain power even after the president's retirement. These individuals become indispensable over time, ensuring their presence even in moments of their retirement or absence.

As a result, workers are constantly dependent on them even for minor decisions. This fuels a sense of pride and conviction that they are the most suitable for the position, as if they are also blue-blooded humans, even though systematically, the system has been adapted to keep them in their places. The incapable ones choose who will replace them, creating a cycle of individualistic dynamics that prevent real social progress.

Often, different cooperatives find themselves in a difficult situation when the president retires, which could lead to their bankruptcy. It seems that he was the only one capable of holding that position and that no one could replace him.

This dependence on a single figure demonstrates a lack of trust in other members of the cooperative and a paternalistic attitude. Instead, everyone should have the opportunity to participate in important decisions, as each is part of the cooperative fabric.

Furthermore, meaningless flattery or praise without meaning only serve to diminish the role of the real protagonists of the cooperative, who are those really in the field facing real services like the OS, the NURSES, and the SANITY MAINTENANCE. Recognizing the value of all those who contribute to success should be a priority, and working together to ensure continuity even after the president's retirement for the common good.

I have had the opportunity, several times, to hear some Presidents boast that after their retirement, there would be no one capable enough to take their place, meaning that they felt they were the only ones suitable to sit in that position.

I wonder, then, what does their statement teach us if not the clearest picture of a lack of transparency?

Therefore, this attitude should be strongly considered devoid of an ethic of social solidarity, all in the name of the democratically established form of the "cooperative."

My personal experiences within cooperatives have allowed me to scratch the surface of the dynamics at play. Often, the president exercises an oppressive power similar to that of past sovereigns, with attitudes that seem outdated and lacking authenticity.

On the other hand, he shows a false attitude of sobriety and a wide fake smile printed on his face. Usually, he does not follow fashion in clothing, and his beard is always messy, a usual symbol of social activism. Personally, I find that this ideology corresponds to an outdated system of deceptive impression.

The Concept of 'Cooperative in a Given Upside-Down Society

We must remember that this country is already a nation where people, by cultural nature, are socially helpful to each other: regardless of the stigma left behind by the division owing to the totalitarian courts of the past. Their history could remind us of this, and the factual evidence is still visible in the reality on the ground, supporting today's Italy after the Second World War. I don't want to retrace the entire history, but I wanted to mention the example of collaboration for the country's reconstruction after the second 'European/Asian war' but call 'world war'. This attitude also represents the fundamental principle of Christianity, of which this country is the cultural champion. In all literature or debate on the canonical functions of cooperatives in a given society, it has always been stated, both in writing and verbally, that cooperatives should focus on user needs, for which services must be satisfied as a primary prerogative. However, little substance is observed in this regard. To explain further, the reason behind the birth of cooperatives was to respond to social challenges in a context of rapid cultural changes. Modern cooperatives were created to focus on assisting those in distress, requiring instances of solidarity. These cooperatives should arise as expressions of civil society to avoid excess bureaucracy and the dynamics of clientelism, classism, and power.

After all that has been said so far, but in my experience, the contrary is the case. Several reasons make the delegation of social services to cooperatives by Public Administration ineffective:

1) One of the main problems is the conflict of interests, both economically and personally;

2) Cooperatives are often forced to adapt to the current local political agenda to survive, at the expense of user needs and the lack of constructive dialogue: this can lead to the deprivation of the rights of needy citizens, with no improvement;

3) The primary goal of the cooperative managers has become to avoid legal problems and accumulate resources in order to participate in tendering competitions;

4) These goals often result in poor service quality offered to needy users without any innovation because they more focus on impressing those that are responsible for the contracts.

In a general situation of social decay, cooperatives often have no ideas on how to improve the situation because of their distance from reality. On the other hand, Public Administration is hindered by politics and often does not participate significantly in solving the most urgent problems. Moreover, it is difficult to distinguish the differences between cooperatives and associations, which often confuse their actions for financial reasons. This leads to a bias against the poor and a lack of competence in social assistance activities. This attitude prevents any possibility of dialogue to find a corrective solution. In this way, our intentions of solidarity become harmful to society and become in vain. "Unfortunately, in today's society, dignity no longer seems to be considered a value in any area of life. This is particularly concerning in sectors where those who should defend and protect the human rights and dignity of the neediest are now using these people as tools for false glorification, in order to acquire more wealth and power needlessly."

I have also noticed that people are comfortable in the comfort zone they have been able to model out for themselves through crook or hook. They have soon forgotten the steep price paid in the past by those who allowed this current, less disturbing and liveable situation in some parts of the world today: what I define as 'The Grandfather Effect.' For me, this psychological situation represents a kind of general guarantee that many active generations today derive from their relatively calm economic situation of the older generation. Thanks to the hard-earned money from grandparents that then constitutes a kind of social security, especially in Italy.

However, this situation is changing, and we can observe already everywhere today, the lower classes are undergoing constant oppression to varying degrees. We must remember that we are all connected, and by acting today, we can prevent the cycle of war from perpetuating in the future. What may seem irrelevant today could become the root of tomorrow's problems. In my opinion, every sustainable project for social solidarity must incorporate financial prudence, community spirit, and human resource management skills. Constant supervision by qualified personnel within public administration is crucial. In any case, we have come back to where we were before, just like a merry-go-round but in a negative form. However, something must be done to make our current situation in this society more sustainable in terms of effective social solidarity.

A Partial Psychocultural Analysis: The "Forged Absolute Knowledge Deficit"

So, I found myself facing a serious psychological problem in today's society. I have undertaken a study and research on a syndrome that I have called the "forged absolute knowledge deficit." This syndrome manifests as self-deception that makes us believe we are acting correctly to adapt to the times while, in reality, we engage in insignificant tasks to avoid truly important ones. It is a form of escape from responsibilities that can lead to a severe knowledge deficit. I have recognized the importance of addressing this syndrome and focusing on activities that truly contribute to our well-being and personal development. This attitude could force anyone to submit indirectly or directly to a more informed person who has more availability in terms of time, coupled with personal effort as a form of a life hero. This mental state has nothing to do with gifts, talents, or intelligence, which are recognized along with intrinsic natural goodness for good reasons. Indeed, this topic requires further exploration.

The Search for Bureaucratic Knowledge Instead of Solidarity by Cooperatives

In the current situation, cooperatives are increasingly accumulating bureaucratic skills to preserve their strategic heritage, which represents a source of profit for the oligarchs. However, there is less attention to issues related to precariousness and critical aspects of the social system. The oligarchs are increasingly engaged in finding new and easy ways to bypass new rules and regulations; to avoid discrepancies regarding their current position and the question of how to set aside a significant sum of funds for themselves. The most plausible reason behind this strategy could be the possibility of the cooperative's failure tomorrow, which means it would not affect their personal wealth. Their operational strategy is based on past experiences that have empirically proven to promote their personal interests. This approach has worked in the past and represents a kind of guideline to maintain their position within the cooperative structure. It is often heard: "Why take risks when everything seems to be going on as expected?". In this way, their strategy is based on stability and bureaucratic security from the past. This seemingly stable situation generates no concerns of any kind and seems to proceed according to the usual pattern.

The Use of Tolerated Exploitation

The cooperative should demonstrate sensitivity to the services it can offer and should also pay attention to the well-being of the workers of its members, in accordance with what is established in the statute. This duty should have at its core the need to promote deep collaboration and fair treatment both in performance and initiatives. It is intended to report that the cooperative cares about the well-being of its members and the community in which it operates, promoting social solidarity and seeking to mitigate the precariousness that might be overlooked by public institutions. At the same time, it should be emphasized that cooperatives were established with the aim of reducing the risk of excessive bureaucratization in public administration and the misuse of social services. A tangible example of a little-known but widespread reality is represented by cooperatives in the North, where there is irregular hiring of laborers in terms of positioning and the exploitation of workers is tolerated. Cooperatives present two distinct aspects: an external one, represented by the services provided, and an internal one, which aims to improve the well-being of members and users as a form of mitigation of social precariousness. This has partly led to the transfer of the management of social services to the cooperative system, thus creating a new centre of power. Thus, a form of secondary civic collaboration could be developed to ensure a more efficient and timely response to threats to the social well-being of society. However, over time, these noble social ideologies have transformed into an even more serious threat to the entire social fabric. Of course, there is an obvious conflict in trying to perform a proper activity as a social cooperative in the absence of specialization or rational handling in terms of cultural complexity, both inside and outside the cooperative itself.

The Cooperative of Applauded Abnormal Entanglements.

Democratically, my reflection is based on the current reality that I have had the opportunity to closely observe. I would like to share my personal experience I had with cooperatives in this country. During my involvement with this cooperative, I had the opportunity to highlight a reality that seems to contradict the fundamental principles that a cooperative should embody. This experience I lived through demonstrates how reality deviates from constitutional aspirations and common beliefs regarding civic cooperation. These aspirations include the importance of evaluating and recognizing the value of the "cooperative" in the society, following the statute and the ethical code that bind affiliated members in service to the community and emphasizing the idea of social solidarity among individuals in the 21st century. What I noticed within the cooperative is the lack of authentic democratic values. I speak of values that go beyond mere words and find concrete expression in the statute, collective participation, voting, and the promotion of social solidarity. Unfortunately, these values seem to be absent within the organization. Cooperative politics are often purely influenced by an oligarchic ideology that denies the presence and adequate recognition of the work done by those who make daily services possible for the society. A particularly surprising aspect was the method of operation aimed at creating a kind of dependency on the part of collaborators. This has the effect of making collaborators feel indebted to the oligarchies and, over time, instilling a sense of loyalty. The entire situation reveals the seriousness of this approach on human psyche. Initially, it seemed that the cooperative would have members with the right skills. However, I noticed that these skills were often underestimated, perhaps to prevent the expertise of these people from highlighting gaps and discrepancies in how the oligarchies are managing the situation in their favour. This attitude aimed to prevent the rise of associated members who did not share the decision-making approach of the oligarchies. Indeed, this approach seemed to aim at limiting the rise of individuals with adequate skills, avoiding that they could gain influence both within and outside the cooperative. This attitude reflects a lack of trust and respect towards cooperative members and their abilities. It would have been wiser to value the skills of cooperative members and work together to achieve common goals, rather than trying to maintain excessive control over people and decisions made. Too often, I noticed the incompetence that characterizes many of the services assigned by public institutions to cooperatives. Bureaucratic justifications often lack meaning, and too often there is a lack of effective control by service centres. I wonder, what would be the purpose of the cooperatives if they did not reinvest in social resources? I think our purpose in life should not only be the accumulation of wealth but rather making a difference. Money itself has no value without a purpose that goes beyond mere profit-seeking.

Duplicate Services between Cooperatives and Public Administration: A Critical Overview

In our current reality, there is evidence of the existence of a significant number of duplicated services operated both by public administration and cooperatives simultaneously, without an apparent logic other than opening a path to illicit gains. Often, services already provided by public administration (e.g., expenses for hiring healthcare professionals who are already present in the public health sector, etc.) are also entrusted to cooperatives through contracts or inserted into other initiatives, causing an overlap of services in terms of funding, expenses, and management complexity.

In some cases, situations arise where a cooperative is assigned a contract without having the expertise or resources to manage the required services. This is particularly evident in sectors like hospitality, where the cooperative might find itself managing services it has no experience with or intention to continue handling except for the sake of easy profit. This behaviour raises questions about the consistency with the ethical and moral ideals underlying the formation of cooperatives, which should aim for solidarity and benefit to the community.

I have noticed several times that many projects are promoted without any apparent logic, driven by those who idolize the president or are part of his family or influential circle. This irrational and antisocial attitude generates negative consequences both for the cooperative and for the community as a whole.

Such decisions are often made by the president but are justified by the apparent support of the board of directors (BOD). This dynamic allows oligarchs to manipulate cooperative funds as they please, exploiting false pretexts.

A frequent tactic is to eliminate associated workers who could pose a threat to their illicit agenda. For example, under the pretext that there are no longer sufficient contracts to justify the continued employment of these workers. This is done using every possible means, such as reducing working hours or assigning less rewarding roles. In this way, they will now be forced to work with those who once worked under their direction and be paid less, and so on. These transfers serve to weaken workers and create a more controllable environment for the oligarchs.

Despite the deceitful operations they carry out, the president always maintains a smile on his face, making his ability to conceal his true intentions even more disturbing.

All the old members of the cooperative have always been in conflict with the president for the authoritarian way he concentrates power and financial matters under his control: from selecting members of the board of directors (BOD) to choosing contracts for instrumental expenses or various maintenance to be assigned to those who are somehow linked to him (for example, the reconstruction of our new cooperative headquarters or even cheaper things to do or buy, like repairs to the organization's vehicles or other).

In summary, the president holds extraordinary authority in choosing recipients for any activity related to economic interest or influence within the cooperative.

Operators of Social Solidarity: In Search of Meaning and Justice

From a broad perspective, it is crucial to consider the concept of "social solidarity" as a fundamental pillar of any society. This principle should act as a mediator that balances power between individual and collective interests, contributing to the sustainable well-being of individuals in an ever-changing social context.

In this article, we will explore some ways in which operators of social solidarity can effectively transform their work into productive action at a time when the future of well-being and culture is at stake. For example, some things we have already learned and know:

1) A key strategy is to create support networks among individuals and communities. These networks can act as a solid foundation on which to build concrete interventions and improvement strategies;

2) Involving young talents in creating projects for the common good is another way to stimulate innovation and collaboration, ensuring a continuous flow of new ideas and solutions;

3) That could contribute and promote reintegration and rehabilitation of various types of those in need in various ways;

4) Furthermore, promoting open and inclusive dialogue among various stakeholders can contribute to dismantling barriers and creating a fertile ground for change.

In summary, a key role of operators of social solidarity is to support and promote the reintegration and rehabilitation of those in need in various forms. This can happen through educational programs, professional training, and access to mental health services. Additionally, working to remove barriers that prevent people from accessing resources, providing information and assistance, is a crucial step to ensure everyone has the opportunity to fully participate in society.

Despite these ideas finding resonance in many discussions, they have often encountered obstacles. Most personalities (the presidents of cooperatives and their privileged representatives) who have been invited everywhere to talk about cooperative issues have always expressed many praises for the well-done work of the cooperatives, responding only to easy requests on television, radio, or social media. But this rhetoric often has not been translated into concrete actions. Instead of tackling complex challenges, some personalities have preferred to avoid detailed discussions, sometimes using banal arguments to avoid sharing uncomfortable truths.

In reality, most of these people do not even know what it means to work under pressure or make drastic decisions in emergency situations, perhaps in the middle of the night, facing unforeseeable circumstances: sometimes between life and death, or in a situation that will determine the existence of another person for their entire life.

Indeed, the nature of the work of operators in social solidarity requires deep involvement and understanding of the real needs of the people. Often, it involves making decisions under pressure and facing critical situations, often in unpredictable circumstances. This deep commitment is what distinguishes those who are truly committed to community improvement. Cooperatives more often systematically deny the needy, i.e., people who are not able to sustain themselves, the right to citizenship and dignity in exchange for compensation. In practice, these people end up becoming "prisoners of the welfare system," hostages of a system that, instead of responding to their needs, treats them as commodities available to the same cooperatives that boast of providing them with a false sense of benevolence. However, the principles of the cooperative itself are often compromised by illicit behaviours and an unequal distribution of power. These leaders often act without fully considering the needs of the needy, and their methods reflect a desire to maintain control and personal interests. Ultimately, a system that does not penalize the needy is needed but helps them concretely and guarantees them full self-determination and dignity. Those who actually do the minimum necessary work to keep the cooperative going, despite the many tensions, are those nameless operators who do their best to satisfy their conscience, while conscienceless leaders are only after profit only for themselves. At the same time, this situation has become a political problem for left-wing parties due to their ideological tendency, which silently makes them pay a price for their goodwill towards the interests of cooperative oligarchs. During my involvement with the cooperative, I tried to emphasize the need for communication, strategic planning, and accountability. This fact-checking process led me to question the behaviour of this organization, seeking an answer to the inefficiencies and problems I have noticed. However, my curiosity was rejected, and I was faced with limitations in my tasks and remuneration. My actions were not motivated by negative intentions but rather by the desire to understand how to improve the functioning of the cooperative. However, I experienced obstacles and refusals from the top, which highlighted further management and power distribution issues within the organization. My experience proves to me that, despite the nice words and praise, the cooperative often does not respect the fundamental values of social solidarity. On the contrary, it can become fertile ground for the perpetuation of personal interests and inequalities. For cooperatives to be truly effective in improving society, it is essential to address these issues and commit to transparency, fairness, and the real well-being of the communities they serve.

Current Examination of Facts and Conclusion Regarding My Collaboration with the Cooperative

In the cooperative, it has become evident that the existing system is neither sustainable operationally nor culturally. Consequently, I decided to undertake a detailed fact-checking mission to fully comprehend the situation. I embarked on this mission with the intent to identify the real issues plaguing the cooperative. Initially, I explored three possible scenarios that were clear in my mind:

1) **Lack of Communication among Members:** One potential challenge could be the lack of communication among cooperative members. If addressed correctly, this aspect could be activated to promote greater cohesion and collaboration within the group.

2) **Absence of an Operational Plan and Executive Strategy:** Another considered perspective is the potential lack of a well-defined operational plan and executive strategy. Implementing these elements could provide clear and rational guidance for cooperative activities, contributing to its stability and long-term success.

3) **Suspicion of Hidden Actions Favouring Oligarchs:** Further reflection, connected to fact-checking, led me to question whether

some observed dynamics are aimed at hiding information from those outside the group, operating in favour of oligarchic interests. This potential dimension may require further investigation and critical examination to fully understand its scope and consequences. In the first place, this attitude betrays the principal objective of cooperation, apart from the egoistical tendency involved.

This last hypothesis raised questions about the transparency of cooperative activities and the integrity of its operations. Throughout my investigation, I sought a deeper understanding of the situation to formulate an accurate conclusion regarding my future involvement with the cooperative.

In conclusion, my current commitment is geared towards a detailed understanding of the factors influencing the cooperative's functionality. My hope is that this fact-checking process leads to concrete solutions and a clear vision for the future of collaboration.

In a nutshell, I decided to take action to explore these options by exclusion. I began requesting meetings with oligarchs to openly discuss some of the very apparent problems afflicting our cooperative. Among these were the irrational management of materials, disproportionate expenses on various projects, and excessive maintenance costs and other unnecessary expenses, just to name a few, rather than meeting pressing social needs.

In some cases, we managed to resolve issues that did not directly interfere with oligarchic interests. However, as soon as it became evident that my investigation could touch on more delicate issues, such as the alleged presence of illicit treasures, oligarchs began avoiding me, advancing unfounded excuses, as previously reported. 'Given my lack of skeletons in the closet,' as they say, my main interest was to understand how the cooperative could be managed to ensure better outcomes for the community. This philosophy became my primary research focus.

However, the oligarchs began excluding me from various cooperative dynamics, limiting my presence in various places where we were developing projects, with the goal of avoiding my encounter with too many people. My working hours were reduced, resulting in lower remuneration. The culmination of this situation occurred in April 2022 when, with labour union support through a settlement agreement, my collaboration was terminated.

My biggest surprise was discovering that the idea of the cooperative as common ownership, based on rights and duties, to which we had always been instructed and which was also formally written in all documents, turned out to be a pure lie. Faced with this situation, we opted for a separation agreement. Before that, I explained my situation to the labour union representative and some lawyers, receiving solidarity but no willingness to take actions that required personal sacrifices from any of them.

This episode would constitute a serious crime against humanity, especially within the context of social solidarity. It seems as though there are hidden forces trying to hinder freedom of information and undermine social justice to preserve their selfish interests.

However, many cooperatives face bureaucratic challenges without suitable tools to address the issues of the precarious social system. The current Italian cooperative system requires greater commitment to improving performance, creating value for members and society as a whole. Close internal and external collaboration, along with public administration, with adequate checks, is essential to equip themselves with the necessary tools and skills to address the challenges of the current social context. Only through constant commitment and a long-term vision will it be possible to overcome difficulties and achieve excellence.

The importance of welfare in a democratic system becomes evident, considering the challenging conditions of disability, poverty, illness, and incarceration not only for those who suffer from them but also for their relatives and loved ones. However, these issues often escape media attention unless they become symbols used by cooperatives to raise funds in the name of the neediest.

EXPLORING THE CONCEPT OF "SOCIAL"

The term "social" should carry profound meaning, conjuring the imagery of cooperation and unity towards a shared objective. However, often this term no longer retains the special connotation that should inspire a respectful attitude. Consider social justice or social solidarity, which should evoke feelings of importance and value. Unfortunately, the excessive and frequently misused use of the word 'social' has diminished its impact. Many cooperative managers are not fulfilling the function or duty for which they were called: addressing the social challenges that characterize their community. Even if no one openly acknowledges it, it doesn't seem right.

Regrettably, the repercussions disproportionately affect the most vulnerable, those without a voice or unions to represent them for their defence. This complex situation is exacerbated by the fact that both government and cooperative elites are detached from social problems, as personal or group interests often take precedence over the efficiency of the entire cooperative system in terms of social issues. The void that cooperatives currently occupy is a crucial space in Italian society. In fact, the inefficiencies highlighted in this book amplify the difficulty of addressing existing complex social problems. In political jargon, it is a "lesser evil," but the reality is that a new model is needed to respond to the emerging demands of social solidarity in the country.

A Perspective on "CULTURE" and Life for Existence

Culture, as defined by various sources, is the set of knowledge, beliefs, values, habits, languages, attitudes, and artifacts shared by a group or society. This set of elements defines the way of life and mentality of a community, outlining its identity and cultural heritage. *If I may be permitted to use a business term, in the simplest form of expression, culture could also be likened to a brand. Culture, similar to a 'brand', represents the identity and values of an organization or community. Just as a brand distinguishes itself from competitors and attracts customers, culture sets an organization apart and attracts individuals who align with its principles.*
Culture is a phenomenon in constant evolution and influences every aspect of communication,

interpersonal relationships, economic activities, and political choices of a nation or region. Culture is expressed through multiple channels, from the arts to music, literature to dance, food to fashion, and in many other forms of creative expression. For this reason, the power that distinguishes a successful living being from a failed one in regards to human conception lies in action taken according to the prevailing conceptual structure in that society. This power to define a society influences individual perspective, ferrying an individual from a personal point of view to a collective one within a shared cultural structure. So, culture means an involuntary acceptance through the annihilation of a living being's point of view to transform it into that of a familiar collective point of view. This process begins with small groups, such as the family, and extends throughout the entire existence of different communities. Ultimately, culture provides a sense of belonging.

However, reducing the study of culture to a single academic field is limiting, as culture is a life lived itself. This is also why we should not blame anyone personally for any attitudinal misbehaviour or blame somebody for the entire problematic situation around us; instead, we should collectively make provisions for mutual resolutive understanding. Certainly, self-awareness helps us find the right place and paves the way for our needs within our capabilities, capacities, and understanding, which will also satisfy

our goals and intentions measured and based on a balanced criterion between us and our nature!
Furthermore, culture has the potential to serve as a bridge between different cultures and promote social inclusion, valuing differences and preserving historical and environmental heritage. It is important to preserve and promote culture so that it can continue to positively influence the world we live in and provide us with a more comprehensive and deeper understanding of life and society. All of this has added value only through the recognition of diversity and the valorisation of cultural differences, not its interpretations, which can be influenced by other forms of ideologies aiming to favour the hegemony of thought. Instead, factual artifact presences should ensure valid sources. It is what we have recognized as our culture that brings us closer to customary belonging. The impact of culture is not limited to the mental and emotional sphere; in fact, culture is not violent on its own because it has no entity presence on its own. Moreover, its chosen deceptional point of assimilation is permissiveness.
Our physical body also reacts to cultural influence in subtle but significant ways. For example, as we approach the weekend, many of us may feel a change in energy and bodily sensation and an awareness in our consciousness of our calendar dating mechanism. This can be attributed to cultural programming in our biological setup that associates the weekend with rest, fun, and relaxation.

In my opinion, therefore, "culture is the study of everything"! This book is also a result of research on facts about social reality, in the collaborative association and interaction together with its main factor in our existence, which is humanity in solidarity.

Contributing to Social Change and Deep Reflections: A Contribution to Social Understanding

In summary, after everything that has been said in this book, in the synopsis, I would like to reiterate as a reminder that my intent was not to defend any form of moral, ethical, or religious superiority. Secondly, my observations do not stem from an egotistical, intellectual, or economic perspective, nor from a craving for the spotlight. I do not claim that my point of view is the only valid one, but I intend to present my clarification based on our prevailing cultural mindset today in our collective memory. Since we don't have any valid concrete evidence of the primordial creation of existence, it will be interesting to consider our understanding within the framework of our cultural context of viable knowledge of the things around us. Therefore, my goal was to defend the social agreements we have made among ourselves based on my interpretation according to cultural and civil canon, as one of the people living together in the same nation and under the same constitution that binds us.

My experience has taught me that it is not enough just to be noticed; it is equally important to listen, speak, and share to give meaning to one's existence. However, this approach might not automatically lead to tangible change unless a divine force intervenes to catalyse the actual change, anyway. So, on the other hand, for me, this situation is linked to my desire to contribute culturally and civically being part of our complex existence as human beings while living in a societal context alongside other people!

This book represents my social testimony, aiming to delve into the concept and further analysis of what 'social solidarity' in our collective memory represents. It focuses on the cultural necessity and to explore this concept in its most basic fundamental perspective, according to my understanding and primarily in its universal definition. I deliberately avoided adopting any kind of intellectual canon to provide a more expository view. Moreover, I am consciously circumventing also any form of bibliography reference to escape the risk of conceptual influences that could divert my attention from the actual critical facts.

This book is primarily based on information that could ignite a sense of responsibility and a reconsideration of any socially based project's tempestuous reform, in relation to the dynamic progression of our society, by those who might be interested in doing so; not only on an educational structure of conceptual use. When it becomes so apparent that some people are stealing what belongs to each of us, but especially what should be destined for the needy, this attitude cannot be stopped by complaining. This situation cannot be ignored or minimized. So, we can avoid "making a bundle of all the grass." Fundamentally, this is the reason why there should be a structure of law and order applicable in a fair and equitable society of public awareness.

My intention was to expose the solid cultural and ethical foundation of social solidarity, a driving force in human relationships, regardless of the historical period we find ourselves in. In any case, when we move through life with a goal, it is important to plan carefully and consider the circumstances around us to decide whether to act calmly or hastily. The key lies in the balance between respect for ourselves, others, and the environment around us.

Only through a correct and rational assessment of our relationship with the environment and other living beings that share this enigmatic life with us can we face the known and unknown with respect and for our well-being. In this way, our conscience can be upright with good intention. However, even with careful planning, we are not perfect in our decision-making process, and we must be tolerant to ourselves and others for the sake of our nature.

This situation has allowed me to understand how we set our goals and how these same goals can also influence our perspectives. Furthermore, I have also learned that every action has its consequences, and judgment also plays a role in the perfection of our actions.

As a result, the whole society and our natural existence can be in harmony with the 'power of creation'. In the end, the power of existence will be manifested as an appeal of judgment at the end of each segment of our action, determining the perspective from which to perfect things.

It is obvious that the political situation of our days is a dirty game. It would be desirable that some existential realities were spared from abuses, especially the neediest among us in a fragile citizenship situation (such as the disabled, the elderly, the sick, prisoners, and the poorest among the poors). Unfortunately, some personalities are doing business in their names.

A Reflection on the Political System: Democracy and Autocracy

From my point of view, the preference for democracy over an autocratic system of government is evident, despite both systems being based on the concentration of power in a few individuals. Democracy allows room for opposition, upholding the principles of freedom of speech and expression, as well as a balance of powers through a system of checks and balances. The focus here is on the possibility to be able to argue and debate issues rather than the outcome of the possibility itself: since that is not the main purpose of this book. Although politics may often seem like a dirty game, it is desirable to preserve the dignity of those who are more vulnerable and in greater need of protection: fragile citizens such as the disabled, the elderly, the sick, detainees, and the less fortunate. Exploiting these categories for personal gain represents a betrayal of humanity within the democratic sphere. From my perspective, democracy, with its ability to allow open debate of ideas and promote the participation of all citizens, represents a beacon of hope for preserving fundamental human values. Its strength lies in protecting rights and safeguarding the dignity of every individual, regardless of their social position or life circumstances.

AUTHOR'S NOTE

The author of this book, of whom I am the same person. So, I present myself as a passionate social activist deeply committed to sustainability in all its facets, making no distinctions in preferences except to respond to the manifested needs in critical moments of our existence. This commitment is outlined within the bounds of my expertise, always rooted in a solid understanding of the anticipated real facts. On the other hand, I adopt a reflective and self-aware perspective as the narrator, refusing to be defined exclusively through recognized successes or experiences of my life, which are often distorted depending on any context, circumstance, place, time, etc., in question, without bringing all these same facts into account to describe my real identity. In this way, as the author of this book, I challenge the conventions of representation based on superficial assessments and biased attitudes related to class or preferences, emphasizing the clear distinction between the art of presentation and the true essence of existence. The information gathered in this book encompasses most of the facts we are aware of regarding cooperatives. Each of us possesses fragmented knowledge of such facts, acquired through different circumstances, entities, times, and spaces. However, to fully grasp the breadth of this information, someone needs to adopt a mindset or a point of view similar to mine to be able to see the situation that I see. This underscores how cultural attitudes subtly influence our lives along our existential journey here on this globe, called Earth.

www.ingramcontent.com/pod-product-compliance
Lightning Source LLC
Chambersburg PA
CBHW050812260726
48660CB00004B/1382